# The Encyclopedia of Kitchen Witchery

## A Beginners Guide to Southern Hemisphere Hedge Magic

### By Cassandra Sage

Cassandra Sage

"A sound soul dwells within a sound mind and a sound body."

— Atsushi Ōkubo

Cassandra Sage

First Edition, 2024

Witch Way Publishing
3436 Magazine Street
#460
New Orleans, LA 70115
www.witchwaypublishing.com

Copyright © 2024 by Cassandra Sage

Editor: Tonya Brown
Copy Editor: Vickie Moua
Cover Designer: Quirky Circe Designs
Illustrator: Haley Newman

All rights reserved. This book or any portion thereof may not be reproduced or used in any manner whatsoever without the express written permission of the publisher except for the use of brief quotations in a book review.

Printed in the United States of America

ISBN Paperback: 979-8-8690-0110-8
ISBN E-Book: 979-8-8690-0111-5

# Table of Contents

| | |
|---|---:|
| Table of Contents | 5 |
| **Part One** | 9 |
| Glossary | 11 |
| The Steps of Spellwork | 15 |
| Introduction | 18 |
| What is a Hedge Witch? | 18 |
| Cooking for Health | 21 |
| Southern Hemisphere Magic | 23 |
| The Alchemist Key | 23 |
| Making Magic | 25 |
| The Ritual of Cooking | 28 |
| A Witch's Garden | 33 |
| General Tips | 34 |
| Indoor Gardens | 36 |
| Greenhouse | 38 |

Outdoor Garden | 40

Conclusion | 42

**Part Two** | 44

Magical Combinations | 46

Pure Joy | 47

Going My Way | 49

Love Boat | 50

Lustful Combinations | 52

Coven Connection | 54

Magic Magnifier | 55

Festive Feasting | 56

Just Vibing | 57

Water Combinations | 58

Fresh Fruit Teas | 62

Shelved Magic and Magical Gifts | 66

Dried Fruit | 68

Herbal Cooking Oil | 69

Flavored Extracts | 70

The Encyclopedia of Kitchen Witchery ● 7

| | |
|---|---|
| Vodka Combinations | 71 |
| Sweet Syrups | 72 |
| Fruit Puree | 73 |
| Herbed Butter | 81 |
| Vinaigrettes | 82 |
| Bottled Fruit | 83 |
| Healthy Combinations | 85 |
| **Part Three** | 100 |
| Herbs and Spices | 101 |
| Vegetables | 148 |
| Fruit | 174 |
| Nuts | 207 |
| Mushrooms | 213 |
| Edible flowers | 220 |
| Miscellaneous | 234 |
| About the Author | 252 |
| Index | 253 |

Cassandra Sage

# Part One

Cassandra Sage

# Glossary

**Activation Bowl:** A bowl decorated with the Alchemist Key, used to activate raw fruits, vegetables, and nuts.

**Alchemist Key:** Sigil representing water, fire, and air. Activates and strengthens the natural magical qualities within food.

**Energy Harnessing:** Also called energy manipulation. It is the basis of all magic and the reason why it works in the first place. We cannot change mana, but we can gather, contain, and move it around. Most of all, we can infuse it with our intention.

**Dream Walking:** It is very similar to astral traveling, but instead of visiting places or people, it is used to interact and communicate with nature and plants. Just as with mild telepathy and certain psychic abilities, the communication received by you will be in the form of feelings, imagery, and sudden knowledge or understanding.

**Centering:** Centering is a practice performed before energy harnessing. It stimulates your mana, allowing it to flow with more ease from you into the magical meal you are creating. Every branch of magic has its own form of centering, including meditation, dancing around bonfires to drums, and the ingestion of hallucinogenics.

**Graveyard Walking:** The ritual of walking through graveyards, taking care, cleaning up, and weeding old or forgotten graves. In exchange you may 'ask' for some of the dirt. Part of the exchange includes leaving flowers, small gifts, or candies and toys when it comes to children. Those who have the talent of spirit talking, otherwise known as 'death stalking', will seek out ghosts or trapped souls with the sole intention of listening. Even if you are not talented in death stalking, talk to the spirits of the graves you are tending. Even if you cannot see them, they enjoy the company.

*Note: Do not bring frankincense or sage into a graveyard.*

**Grounding**: Sometimes performing rituals can leave us feeling over stimulated, making us jittery and shaky, with a heightened sense of awareness. Grounding is a technique used to calm your mana.

**Lucid Dreaming:** Being 'awake' within your dream (i.e., knowing that you have entered the dream realm). The more accomplished can control aspects of the dream.

**Manifestation:** Bringing your wants and desires to fruition through visualization techniques, including regularly entering a hypnotic or meditative state and 'visualizing' the desired event and outcome.

> **TIP:** *Give a gift or sacrifice to nature before attempting to manifest something great. This can be something physical like planting a tree; or time spent helping at places such as your local animal shelter. The magical karma will aid you in what you are trying to achieve.*

**Mutual Dreaming:** A dream shared with another. This occurrence is easier to accomplish when you have experience with lucid dreams, and have a close bond with the other dreamer.

**Mana:** Mana is the universal life force and energy current that flows through us and through everything else. Also called or referred to as qi, chi, vibration, auras, and natural energy (See Chapter on Fruit).

**Psychic Awareness/Ability:** Labeled by scientists as extra sensory perception or ESP. This branch of magic includes a list of abilities including astral travel, automatic writing, bilocation, levitation, telepathy, and fortune telling.

**Shielding:** Shielding is the term for protecting yourself and your mana from the likes of negative energy, including psychic, mental and magical attacks.

**Sympathetic Magic:** Also referred to as imitative magic, is the attempt to change fate though mimicking the desired event. Examples of this are rain dancing and voodoo dolls.

**Tulpamancy:** A tulpa is a being or creature created through visualization and energy harnessing. What begins as imagination, turns into something tangible and sentient. Tulpas make wonderful companions, friends, and guardians against entities from the spirit realms, demonic forces, and Fae. With enough effort, close knit covens can show and introduce their tulpas to one another. Strong covens have been known to share in a tulpa creation, creating a messenger and single guardian for everyone involved.

Cassandra Sage

# The Steps of Spellwork

Before delving into the world of kitchen witchcraft, it is crucial to understand the basic steps of performing any spellwork. Most traditions consider it crucial to learn these before practicing any form of magic. Techniques vary depending on what type of craft you are practicing, and it is encouraged to add your own personal touches and traditions where you see or feel fit.

Consider spellwork the same way you would a new recipe. By not preparing, you might find yourself without the correct ingredients or tools; by not concentrating you may miss a step, potentially creating a flop instead of something delicious. The great thing about recipes is that once we are practiced and comfortable with them, we can change them up and put our own new wonderful spin on them.

This is done because a large entirety of spellwork is visualization. Visualization works in stages to maximize its efficiency (i.e., putting an oven on at the beginning of a recipe instead of just before you need to put the cookies in to bake).

### Centering

This would be part of the last precooking checklist phase.

You have the ingredients, and you know what you are going to do with them. Now we lay everything out, make sure our tools are ready, and open the recipe book to the right page.

Centering is the step in which we both mentally prepare and focus ourselves on the task we are about to perform. We create a state of mind needed to perform magic.

This forms part of your opening ceremony.

### Shielding

We use oven gloves to protect our hands from being burnt, and wear aprons to protect our clothes. And just like in cooking, we need to protect ourselves when practicing witchcraft.

Shielding is a way to protect yourself from psychic, mental, or magical attacks. Shielding is not only performed before or part of spell casting; those that are emotionally sensitive to the feelings of others, or have an ability to communicate with the supernatural, use shielding techniques often as a way of protecting themselves.

### Energy Harnessing

Consider this the energy, effort, focus, and love, you put into turning a recipe and a handful of ingredients into a delicious creation.

Energy harnessing is the act of stimulating and utilizing mana to manifest our desires, or the outcome of the magical act or spellwork.

### Grounding

This comes at the end of the meal, and is usually the part we don't enjoy: cleaning up and packing away. It is something that must be done to avoid the consequences. For if we do not pack away leftover food, it would spoil and go to waste. And leaving scraps out would only attract insects, not to mention the visual eyesore of a dirty kitchen.

When we perform energy harnessing, we stimulate, and thereby increase not only our own mana levels, but the mana in everything around us. We might not use all that energy, and it may leave us feeling hyper or in a state of intense awareness, so we use grounding techniques to absorb what we can and disperse the excess.

That is why grounding is done after energy harnessing, and forms part of your closing ceremony.

# Introduction

Welcome to *The Encyclopedia of Kitchen Witchery*, the perfect guide to everyday ingredients, and how to use them.

While this type of magic was originally and primarily known as 'women's magick', it was only because women were primarily responsible for the preparation and cooking of meals. The cooking experience was a great way for a circle of women—or coven—to bond. The natural grace and organizational thinking women have when working as a team in the kitchen stimulates the flow of mana or *magic*; creating for even more brilliant and powerful outcomes.

And if you are not a whizz in the kitchen or find spices and herbs a smidge intimidating, don't fret! This book provides brief explanations on what dishes are best used with your magic ingredients.

> *The knowledge in this book was passed down from mother to daughter, and eventually from my mother to me. Now I pass it on to you. Throughout the book you will find a handful of her anecdotes. Unlike the rest of her knowledge on kitchen witchery, these anecdotes were passed down through storytelling and never before written down, until now.*

## What is a Hedge Witch?

The term *Hedge Witch* stems from the hedges that healers and witches used to grow around their property, giving them easy access to the ingredients they needed (not to mention privacy from prying eyes). Nowadays, easy access to herbs and spices from our local supermarkets allows those that do not have a green thumb an opportunity to practice this style of magic. It is also, in part, the reason why the term *Hedge Witch* fell away, and the term *Kitchen Witch* was popularized in its place.

This makes kitchen witchery one of the oldest of magicks, existing in some form or other, even before the existence of cauldrons and kitchens. There are three sides to this magic:

## Mind

Sights, smells, textures, and tastes of natural ingredients, whether fresh or dried, can positively influence mood, stress, and working capacity. This intern stimulates your spiritual energy or *mana*, which is what you use, or tap into, when performing witchcraft. The sounder and more balanced the mind, the stronger the spiritual energy.

## Spirit

The intangible part of ourselves; our very essence.

But what is the spirit composed of? It has many names, including mana, qi, chi, prana, the life force, energy, and vibrations. It is found within everything: humans, animals, plants, earth, water, etc. It is also the source of our magic.

Kitchen witchery is about stimulating the spiritual energy found within ingredients, thereby activating the magical capabilities for us to harness.

We do this by imbuing the ingredients with our own mana. The healthier a kitchen witch's mana is, the more stimulated the magical properties are within the ingredient. This contributes to how powerful the magical dish is, and the speed of the outcome.

On the other hand, these same ingredients can do wonders in aiding health and defending against sickness. If you are cooking solely for health benefits, focus your thoughts, intentions, and energy during the cooking process on the outcome of good health and healing.

In the chapter about fruit we broach the subject on oxidative stress and how it impacts you, your body, and your spiritual well-being.

## Body

Other ways to naturally increase and stimulate your mana is through exercise. A healthy body increases the effectiveness of your magic. Moreover, a stronger, more physically fit body means magic takes less of a toll, and you will use less energy while still achieving the desired effect.

This does not mean hours of your day need be wasted away with exercise, a simple twenty-minute walk every day can increase your energy and magical capabilities by ten-fold.

## Infusing Food with Magic and Good Energy

Whether you are cooking with magical purpose or for health, for yourself or for others, you must have an end result in mind when choosing your ingredients.

There are a few things one must take into consideration when purchasing ingredients. Try to purchase locally. If not a local farmer, aim for something produced within your own country. While it is not always an option, make a conscious effort to do so whenever possible. When it comes to meats, dairy, fish, and poultry products, make certain that they are free range products and sourced from a humane abattoir. And make sure that your more exotic ingredients, like cocoa and honey, are ethically sourced. All these things add to or detract from the quality of energy coursing through the ingredients.

Just as surroundings and events effect our vibrations, the same can be said for the ingredients we cook with.

The Encyclopedia of Kitchen Witchery • 21

Ingredients sourced unethically will have negative energy attached to it, which is no good for cooking. Buying imported products when you have local farmers producing the same item will have an impact on a more karmic level. Even ancient cultures made sure the animals they hunted did not suffer more than necessary, and they thanked the animals for their sacrifice, as a way of showing respect to the circle (or gods) of life and death.

## Cooking for Health

The original hedge witches were also called upon for magical solutions to daily problems. Before the time of doctors, people would seek out hedge witches, or what they called 'wise- women', to prescribe them herbal remedies and suitable diet for their ailments.

> "People would visit a local Wise-Woman to treat their illnesses and injuries. The Wise-Woman would create her remedies from things she could find in the local landscape: plants, animals, water and minerals like salt." (Museum of Cambridge; Wise Women: Traditional Cures and Remedies)

- *While each ingredient listed does have medicinal properties, herbs and spices are no replacement for a doctor or sound medical advice.*
- *If you are entertaining guests, always remember to ask about allergies. Even the best intentions will be ruined by a trip to the emergency room.*

*Tip: There is no harm in cooking a dish for both health and magical benefits.*

Here are a few tips on how to retain most of the nutritional value from your ingredients during the cooking process:

- ✿ Include the skins of fruit, vegetables, and chicken whenever possible.
- ✿ Avoid boiling.
- ✿ Use minimal liquids.
- ✿ Grilling and baking meats and vegetables are always preferable to frying.
- ✿ Avoid reheating food.
- ✿ Sauté vegetables whenever possible.
- ✿ Minimize the exposure of cut ingredients to air. Don't wait too long between preparing the ingredients and adding the ingredients.
- ✿ Minimize your cooking time for vegetables, fruits, and fresh herbs. The shorter the cooking time, the fewer nutrients are lost.

### Eating Raw

*The magic of an activation bowl.*

If you already enjoy a healthy diet, there is a chance you already appreciate raw fruits, nuts, and vegetables. It would seem quite a hassle to set the mood and perform a closing ceremony if you just wanted to eat an apple or carrot stick. There is a simple solution for this: An activation bowl.

Traditionally, this bowl was made of wood or clay, or woven, but you can choose any bowl that speaks to you. Do consider that certain styles allow for more airflow which helps keep produce fresher for longer.

Somewhere on the bowl, paint, carve or burn the sigil of the *Alchemist Key (see pg. 22).* Then place the bowl in the sun for seven days.

The activation bowl will help activate the magic within your foods, but unlike cooking where you add your energy into the mix, the magic will be milder.

## Southern Hemisphere Magic

*Its origins and how it differs from Northern Hemisphere magic.*

Most of the Southern Hemisphere was colonized at some point in history, primarily by countries lying in the Northern Hemisphere.

When these men on boats landed on the shores with the intention of building a new home in a foreign land, they usually brought women with them. These wives, daughters, and sisters would come together, helping to create new communities, and sometimes building new languages. They shared with each other secrets, food, spices, herbs, work, homes, and lives. And some of those women had brought their own magic from their homelands across the seas, which they shared that too.

They considered Northern Hemisphere magic to be a strict magic. It followed the moon and the stars, its followers sought balance and needed energy and much patience when preparing. But these were new lands, lands of the sun and of chaos. They soon discovered that trying to bring balance to chaos was as futile as trying to swim your way out of a rip tide (The trick to both is to not fight it, but to rather go with the flow.). So, they gathered, sorted through their combined knowledge, and created new magicks, including their own form of hedge magic.

## The Alchemist Key

Food comes from the earth; therefore it is no surprise to discover that all natural foods represent the earth element. When we activate the magic within, we add water, air, and/or fire during the cooking process. Once more than one element is combined, it turns into a new element, which is called *void* by some. *Void* is the strongest of the elements (real world examples of void elements are volcanoes that are both fire and earth, and tropical cyclones that are both water and wind).

While the history of who created the Alchemist Key is lost, we do have understanding on what the sigil represents: the three elements. Air. Fire. Water.

Using this sigil will add the energy of any, or all three, missing elements to your magical meals.

It was also designed to help witches channel their mana. You can carve it into wooden spoons (This is especially helpful for those new to kitchen magic or doubtful of their own ability to activate the magical properties of food while cooking), paint it on your favorite mixing bowls, or sandblast it into your favorite ovenproof dishes.

Or the symbol can be placed on magically activated bottled foods like chutney, jams and preserved fruits, to increase strength of magic within naturally over time. Even your personal recipe book of magical recipes can benefit from having the Alchemist Key on its cover, or scribbled on the front page.

And its use is not limited to the kitchen. Use this symbol in cohesion with the making of natural remedies, mixing essential oils, and creating beauty products, with natural ingredients. You can even carve the Alchemist Key into store bought or self-made candles made from soy, beeswax, or 100% vegetable fat; preferably with a paper, cotton, hemp, or wood wick.

## Making Magic

A little further on, we will provide you with some easy steps to follow, but they are not set in stone. If you are already a practicing witch, we recommend incorporating any elements of your own practiced rituals where you see fit. This style of Southern Hemisphere magic has very few rules, and even those rules are flexible. Go with what feels natural.

> *My mother used to say that instead of a wand, a kitchen witch uses a wooden spoon.*

Cassandra Sage

Here are a few tips to consider before getting started:

- ✿ Consider the magical outcomes you are pursuing by creating this dish or meal, and question whether they are being used with the best of intent.
- ✿ Be sure you have all your ingredients, utensils and kitchen tools, and any recipes you may be using, ready beforehand.
- ✿ You should not be hurried. So, carve out enough time for your ritual.
- ✿ Make sure you are comfortable, with the option of removing your shoes.
- ✿ Visualization and focus are key. Try to lessen outside distractions and intruding thoughts that might pull your focus.

There are three parts to the process, and we start off with the mood, atmosphere, and headspace needed to perform magic. This is followed by the cooking ritual and act of energy harnessing. We end with the clearing up and closing ceremony.

## Creating the Mood

As with any form of magic, you must get into the right headspace in order to get the energy flowing, and put aside outside worries. In magic this is called *centering*; a practice done before energy harnessing. Most branches of magic have their own centering techniques and tradition. For this branch of magic there are four very easy steps to follow:

1. Breath:
   Many centering techniques include some form of meditation, because concentrated breathing helps relax the mind and creates a state of tranquility. Face your workspace, close your eyes, and take several deep breaths to get the energy flowing.

   **TIP:** If you struggle, give the Box Breathing Technique a try. Breath in for four counts, hold for four counts, breath out for four counts, and hold for four counts. Repeat.

2. Set the tone of the meal, and the prep work:
   This can be done with music. Some people like to light candles, pour a glass of wine, or dance, or sing to the music, etc. to get themselves into the right state of mind. Do whatever feels natural, and appropriate for the situation to achieve the mood you are looking for. You can even add or create some of your own customs. This step not only stimulates your mana, but that of the universal and chaos energy that surrounds us.

3. Cleansing is of tantamount importance:
   Clean your workspace and whatever fruit, vegetables, and fresh herbs you may be using. Cleaning is a very good time to visualize the meal creation and envision exactly what you will be doing. Cooking is a sensory art form, so don't only visualize the intentions behind each spice or herb chosen, but engage in your other senses as well.

Imagine the smells each ingredient will conjure when added to your dish; how your tongue perceives each ingredient to taste, before and after; the feel of the ingredients beneath your fingers; in your mind's eye see yourself chopping, peeling cutting, cooking, serving, and sitting down to eat; picture the atmosphere at the table and feel the saliva in your mouth start to gather as you imagine yourself taking that first bite.

4.  <u>Measure out your ingredients and set out your tools beforehand</u>:
    This is when you show silent gratitude to each item as they are the objects of focus. Thank each magical ingredient you use for the magic they add to your meal.

## The Ritual of Cooking

The cooking process and time is when we perform energy harnessing. Here are a few tips before you get started:

- When you cut, chop, prepare, add, and stir your specially chosen ingredients, remember to focus on the reason behind your choice.
- Always stir clockwise, preferably with a wooden spoon.
- Have fun. Relax. And enjoy the cooking experience. You can taste when someone cooks with love and vigor.

Below you will find three events or situations that would influence your cooking ritual. Take note of these as they each have a different purpose:

**Daily Cooking (Low Effort)**

This method is perfect for solitary or single practitioners, as well as for those cooking for a family unit or loved ones. Some find that using a predetermined recipe to be unfitting in this case, and might even choose herbs, spices and fresh ingredients based on what is appealing to the nose or how their day went. It might be as simple as making a cup of tea, or a daily occurrence such as preparing dinner for the family.

Daily rituals are good for beginners because you usually only pick one to three elements to focus on. Common choices are things like love, luck, health, and happiness, which are all things people want an abundance of in life.

Once you have chosen which elements to focus on, create yourself a simple mantra to think or say over and over while you prepare ingredients and cook. Don't make it overly difficult. Remember that you might step away while the food is bubbling away on the stove or baking in the oven, so you want a mantra that is easily remembered and spoken. e.g. Health, wealth, happiness. Mantra's help with focus, and to focus your mana.

## Cooking for Occasions (Medium Effort)

This includes celebrations, festivals, religious ceremonies, and holidays. And it is encouraged to celebrate every occasion, event, and passing of time. From milestones like birthdays and anniversaries, to harvest and full moon, or a Sunday lunch with family, or a dinner party with friends. There is never a poor excuse to observe this variation of cooking ritual.

These sorts of occasions are usually planned ahead of time. If you don't feel like doing all the hard work by yourself, your planning phase is also the perfect time to gather your coven, or a close group of friends, to include in the process. Get together beforehand, decide on the recipes, ingredients, and intentions. Cooking a magical meal with others invites a different level of energy to your dishes. Each person might make a separate dish, or everyone can share the responsibility of preparing all the dishes; the important thing is inclusion.

That said, it matters not if you are a large coven, a couple, or a private practitioner, there is no minimum amount of people needed to observe a special occasion.

Just remember to focus your intentions when working with the ingredients and doing the actual cooking; the rest of the time, enjoy the festivities!

One way this ritual differs from the Daily Cooking ritual is that an outdoor fire is built. It can be a fire pit, bonfire, or brazier; or it can be built for the purpose of direct grilling or potjie food (similar to gumbo, a cast iron cauldron is placed directly over flame).

Traditionally, men would work the fires and take care of food being cooked over the flames, while women were in the kitchen. Another tradition was to ingest or smoke psychoactive herbs, mushrooms, or alcohol, and dance around the fire after. The former tradition is outdated and not something enforced; and the latter is completely optional and a personal choice, and only to be done in a responsible manner.

One of the initial purposes of a fire being lit for celebratory occasions was, and still is, to draw the attention of the gods, magical spirits, or djinn. After the meal was concluded, any bones, scraps, and natural waste left over from the meal creation, is thrown directly into the fire. This is seen as sacrifice, thanking any being that might be attending for their presence and possible blessing.

Incorporate your own beliefs of gods into the above. If you do not have a deity or pantheon, think of it as a signal fire to the universe, signaling your gratitude. Allow everyone to throw their own scraps into the fire. Take this moment to be thankful for whatever it is you are celebrating, and for those you might be sharing the celebration with.

**TIP**: If for any reason you are unable to have an outdoor fire, or if you are hosting the event indoors, a fireplace or candles will do just fine. Just be sure to bury any scraps outdoors.

## Cooking for a Charge (High Effort)

When someone is in need, a witch has a choice to help or not. Once the decision to help is made, that someone becomes a witch's charge. This makes you responsible for them and it is an endeavor not to be taken lightly.

Most charges will come to you for a solemn reason, take note of this when setting the mood for your magical creation.

There is more preparation involved when it comes to cooking for a charge. The first is to determine what they want versus what they need. And we do this through listening and empathy.

Your ingredients and recipes are picked with care.

As with daily cooking, create an easy to use mantra. While you use the mantra, conjure mental imagery and emotions of the outcome you want for your charge. This is where your empathy and understanding of their situation comes in handy.

**NOTE:** Once you have accepted someone as your charge, you have a cosmic and karmic responsibility to them. Be sure to check in with them to see how they are coping, doing, or healing up.

**NOTE**: And a reminder that natural and magical remedies can only go so far. When it comes to mental and health problems, do not be afraid to refer your charge to a medical professional.

### Clearing up and Closing Ceremony

Some people like to clean while they cook, and this is fine. You can perform the closing ceremony with whatever packing away, dirty dishes, and other cleaning is left after the meal. Your closing ceremony is just as important a part as the mood setting and the actual magical cooking and baking.

1. Set your mood as you did in the beginning, or do as you normally would do with your closing ceremony, or a bit of both, as long as it feels right to you. Then begin to clean

and pack away, leaving your counters and stove tops till last.

2. Allow your thoughts to dwell on the smells and taste of the meal you had and those you might have shared it with.

3. Take a moment to be thankful for each ingredient used and the magic you are bringing into your life or the lives of those you shared it with. Be sure to be as specific as possible.

4. As you complete the ritual by wiping down your counter and stove tops, and drying and packing away the now clean dishes, be thankful for your kitchen and the safety it provides for you to do your magic; be thankful for your utensils and tools, for they acted as your wand, a conduit, passing your energy and intentions into the food as you cooked.

5. Finally, look around your clean space, and allow yourself a moment's praise for a job well done. Be thankful to your hands for the meal you prepared, your mind for the thoughts to infuse, your tongue for words and feelings spoken over the food while cooking. And lastly, your heart for those who cook without passion, might as well serve dirt, for it will have the same amount of magical energy.

There is no need for shielding techniques; the level of energy you put into creating your magical dishes is mostly and almost immediately replaced due to the chaotic energy flowing during creation of the meal. And if there is any energy that still needs replacing, it will come from the meal you have prepared.

No one likes the jittery after effects of energy harnessing. The clearing up and closing ceremony works as a grounding ceremony to counter this, but chaos energy usually reabsorbs any excess mana long before.

If you are not planning to partake in the meal, but feel your energy levels are a little lacking, a spoonful of pure honey under the tongue or a piece of fruit from your activation bowl will do the trick.

## A Witch's Garden

A witch's garden can be immaculate with neat little rows, or wild with everything higgledy-piggledy, or an indoor garden to accommodate for space, or simply to fill their home with the energy of nature. Obviously, there are more magical benefits to having an outdoor garden, because you are physically closer to nature.

Whatever you choose, let it be an expression of you and your energy. And as your energy changes over time, so will your garden. The deeper your connection to the garden and the magical ingredients it produces, the stronger the magical outcome when used in cooking.

This chapter provides some basic hints on how to go about creating your own witch's garden.

## **General Tips**

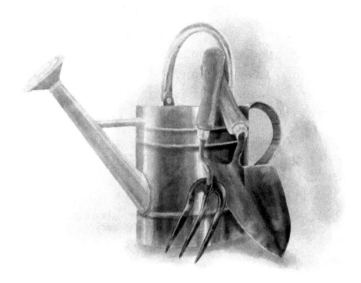

Always do a little research on the plants you intend to grow, and find out what environment, soil, and water requirements they need.

Graveyard dirt, obtained through graveyard walking can be scattered loosely over the top layer of soil. It enhances the magical qualities of everything that grows. It also protects your garden and home from curses, dark spirits, or negative energies. It's best to collect the dirt yourself.

Decorate your garden with statues and art that speak to you. They can be statues of spirits, monsters, or guardians; or shrines that represent gods, Fae, or other spirits; or pieces that stir a specific feeling within you. The more energy you put into your garden, the better the magic within the plants will react to you when used in magical dishes.

Talk, sing, or both, not just to the herbs, but to the nature spirits or Fae that are attracted to, and perhaps live, in your garden.

Take time to hug a tree. It does wonders for your mana and spiritual wellbeing.

Celebrate the solstices (and incorporate your own festivals, rituals, and holidays), and show your garden gratitude by way of a gift or offerings, such as crushed nutshells, eggshells, or ground up hemp or cannabis seeds. You can also gift each plant and tree (or just your favorites if you have a big outdoor garden) with a thank you note written on recycled or rice paper, buried under the soil.

Mirrors are a good way to keep dark energy and negative spirits out of your garden and home. Keep in mind that the sun reflecting off of its surface can burn nearby plants or items.

Have a quiet spot in the garden or near the plants, even if it's just a chair, where you can spend time meditating, reflecting, sewing, being creative, or reading. The stimulated energy generated from these activities is absorbed by the surrounding foliage and increases your connection to the plants.

Use moon and sun water regularly. Set a filled watering-can where it can stand in the rays of the moon or the sun. For a supercharged version, set a watering-can out before daybreak on the first day of full moon. Leave it there to be charged by the full moon and sun for three days and three nights.

Compost bins are a must have. Toss in vegetable and fruit peels and waste, such as teabags, recycled paper like egg cartons, newspaper torn into strips, plant trimmings, fallen leaves, and grass cuttings. These things break down, giving you plant food that is high in nitrogen and moisture.

# **Indoor Gardens**

Most indoor gardens are aimed at fresh herbs, and you will need to plan according to the space you have to make sure there is enough natural light (six to eight hours).

Hanging pots and installing shelves will give you more space. If your garden is near the window, consider a window box inside and outside.

Choose your herbs carefully. Pick the easy to grow herbs (and the ones you plan on using most often):

- ✿ Rosemary
- ✿ Basil
- ✿ Parsley

- ✿ Chives
- ✿ Mint
- ✿ Oregano
- ✿ Thyme
- ✿ Cilantro
- ✿ Lemon Grass
- ✿ Sage
- ✿ Bay Laurel
- ✿ Garlic
- ✿ Lavender

Wherever possible, don't spend money on new pots. Recycle what you have, things like mason jars, cookie or biscuit tins, odd or chipped cups and saucers, old teapots, tin cans, muffin tins, etc. Remember to consider each herb's drainage requirements before planting. And remember something to catch the water that comes from drainage! Be creative wherever possible, even if it is just adding a ribbon.

If you have animals or little children, and perhaps worried of spills and messes, consider a terrarium.

Speak to your local garden center about the right soil to go with your herb selection. If you don't have a green thumb or have no patience for seeds, ask them about seedlings available.

Make sure about the space requirements for your chosen selection to avoid needing to rearrange them at a later stage.

You want liquid fertilizer.

Rule of thumb for watering: Stick a finger in the soil. If the soil is dry, water thoroughly.

Rotate every couple of days so that all sides of the plant get some sunlight.

Temperature should be around 60 to 70 degrees Fahrenheit or 16 to 22 degrees Celsius.

Airflow is important.

Don't overharvest and try to pluck leaves from the bottom first.

## **Greenhouse**

The upside to building a greenhouse is that you have a lot more options with regards to what you can grow and extend your growing season. As long as you take into account plant space needs, temperature, light, and natural pest control.

It is important to find the right spot for your greenhouse. It will need to be a flat surface with maximum exposure to natural light and sunshine, secure from cold wind and potential frost pockets.

Don't cram in too many pots or grow bags. It's easy enough to say you will move them around as the plant requires space, but

The Encyclopedia of Kitchen Witchery • 39

it's not really. They become heavy, and some plants bulky, while others really don't like being moved around.

Always have a thermometer.

You can build shelves and add hanging gardens for more space.

Start with seeds rather than seedling or cuttings.

Here is a list of ingredients that grow well in a greenhouse:

- ✿ Kale
- ✿ Lettuce
- ✿ Mustard greens
- ✿ Carrots
- ✿ Beets
- ✿ Peas
- ✿ Broccoli
- ✿ Asparagus
- ✿ Catnip
- ✿ Mint
- ✿ Rosemary
- ✿ Sage
- ✿ Thyme
- ✿ Parsley
- ✿ Cilantro
- ✿ Basil
- ✿ Seedless cucumber
- ✿ Eggplant
- ✿ Hot peppers

Ventilation is important.

Screen doors aid in pest control and help keep pets out.

Collect rain, moon, and sun water, to use whenever possible.

Don't forget about the roots! Without strong roots, many of your plants won't make it, they also need adequate space to grow.

## **Outdoor Garden**

The outdoor garden is where a hedge witch can truly get the most out of the gardening experience and the end results. An outdoor garden is not only about the potential magical ingredients that can be grown, or having your own safe haven to escape to. It is a place where you can directly absorb the mana flowing from the earth. It is a space for you to create a haven for wildlife, a way of giving back to nature.

    The most important thing when planning your garden, is to make sure that the garden will thrive when you are no longer around. Treat your garden the way you would a child: you help it grow to the point where it can take care of itself.

Unless you are an avid gardener or were born with a green thumb, talk to an expert at your local gardening center. Find out what requirements there are with regards to soil and weather patterns.

Avoid exotic plants at all costs. When choosing plants, make sure they are indigenous to your area, as invasive species can wreak havoc on local plant and wildlife.

When evaluating your garden, take note of where the light falls. Mark out which spots receive sun, shade, or a combination of the two. Different nature spirits live in light versus shade. Some refer to them as the courts of Seelie and Unseelie. And then you have your halflings that crave or tolerate both light and shade. To gain the favor of these nature spirits, plant your garden accordingly. Place plants that love the light in the light. Plant plants and mushrooms that love the dark in the dark. And everything that is in between, plant in the in-betweens.

Do not limit yourself to only planting things you can consume. Plant for beauty, delightful smells, and for the benefit of nature.

Plant marigolds between your vegetables, herbs, and edible flowers. They will attract ladybugs, who in turn will help protect your garden and crops from other insects. If you find ladybirds to be lacking, purchase bags of frozen ladybugs from your local garden center and release them into your garden.

Make an effort to plant food for pollinators like bees and butterflies. Place decorative mini beehives in your garden, and they will come. Just make sure the hive is out of the way from animals and people, especially those with allergies.

During late spring and early winter, when food is scarce, you can always help them out with a little sugar water. **NOTE: DO NOT USE BROWN SUGAR**. This will cause the bees to get very sick. Instead, use two parts white sugar and one part water.

Use a saucepan to heat the water and melt the sugar. If it gets very cold, approximately 50 degrees Fahrenheit and below, the bees might prefer the sugar granules to the water.

When it comes to butterflies, there are other ways to attract them besides flowers. You can use overripe fruits like oranges, strawberries, peaches, mangos, kiwis, and watermelon. Either place on plates with water, or cut up and hang on hooks or tree branches. Butterflies are attracted to the colors red, yellow, orange, pink, and purple, and prefer blossoms that are flat-topped or clustered with short flower tubes. So, keep this in mind when seeking out good nectar sources for them. They also love sun, so try plant and place your butterfly food sources in a place they will receive full sun from mid-morning to mid-afternoon.

Put out bird feeders to attract these musical winged friends.

It is not just the flying creatures we want to attract. Due to humans destroying their habitats and food, much of the local wildlife suffers. As practitioners and children of nature, we should take it upon ourselves to care for these creatures. Besides some happy animals, it would amaze you what interaction with wild animals on a daily basis can do for your mental health and spiritual energy, even if the interaction is limited to watching. Make a list of local wildlife in your area. Aim to add plants they eat or nest in. As for fruit eating animals like squirrels, monkeys, and some foxes, place a feeding station at the end of your garden and put out food for them.

# Conclusion

Southern Hemisphere style kitchen witchery is a loving and forgiving art form. Like most things in life, the more you practice, the better you get it. And because we need food and drink for nourishment, we can easily incorporate this form of magic into our daily lives.

Your kitchen is your altar, a place of ritual, where you can find solace and solitude; a place you can create new and lasting memories; a place full of potential magic and healing. So wherever possible, let your personality shine through, whether you prefer neat and modern, or enchanting and rustic, or anything in-between. Let it be a reflection of who you are.

It doesn't have to happen overnight, you could start small by adding a candle, hanging an art piece, or painting sigils on a tea pot or a clay bowl that will be the center piece to your kitchen table. The possibilities and ideas are endless.

Just as your kitchen is unique to your taste and preference, incorporate your personal beliefs and uniqueness to make this magic your own. Experimentation is encouraged, as is following your gut and your nose. If you are new to practicing magic of any sort, why not do a little research about your local magical history, legends, and superstitions; you might be surprised what speaks to you.

Cassandra Sage

# Part Two

The Encyclopedia of Kitchen Witchery • 45

## Magical Combinations

Combining magical elements and flavors may seem daunting, but the best way to learn is through experimentation. This chapter provides a few examples on how to get you started.

While there are one or two recipes included, below you will mainly find combinations to get your creativity flowing and encourage you to create your own unique magical recipes. By being creative, we hyper-stimulate our spiritual energy, which provides for stronger magic.

These lists of magical combinations are here to stimulate the senses and inspire dishes that will impress your guests.

Each ingredient comes with a brief explanation as to why you are using it and what magic ability you are activating during the cooking process. It also gives you a good idea of how to word your wants and intentions when you create recipes of your own. For a more detailed view on what each ingredient can do—both magically and health wise— make use of the detailed index in part three of this book.

As explained in the introduction, these wants are spoken (or cast via thought), over the food while you are prepping and cooking, and especially while you are stirring. So, the more concise and focused your thoughts, the better your energy is channeled; the better and stronger the magical outcome.

Remember that you can always add more spice and flavor, but you can't take it out once it has been added. So, it's better to err on the side of caution. Also, feel free to add or remove elements as you see fit.

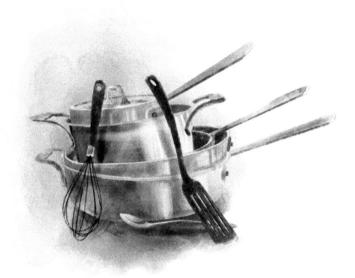

## Pure Joy

Winter months, rainy days, and poor weather can cause melancholy, sadness, irritability, and be the root of many fights among family or friends. Pick one or more of these warm combinations to chase away the cold that has settled inside and give the spirit a boost.

The happier you are, the better your flow of energy and magic. The better your flow of energy, the better your health and creativity. Not to mention, the stronger and more concise your magic will be.

## Base Combination

(This base combination works well with chicken and pumpkin dishes.)

- o 1 Part Nutmeg to attract abundance.
- o 2 Parts Cinnamon to warm hearts.

## Root Vegetable Side Dishes

Add the following to the Base Combination listed above:

- o Maple syrup to taste, to encourage happiness.
- o 1 Part cloves to drive away the loneliness.
- o Your choice of root vegetables e.g., Carrots, sweet potatoes and turnips are a delicious mix. See which intentions suit your current needs best.

## Curry Dishes

Add the following to the Base Combination listed above:

- o 1 Part Anise seed for happiness.
- o Minced beef (optional) to lessen aggression and encourage a blissful feeling.
- o Tumeric (for yellow rice) for vitality.

## Hot Cacao/Cocoa

Add the following to the Base Combination listed above:

- o Cacao/cocoa to taste, for feelings of compassion and love.
- o Milk to help us remember better times and how fleeting the bad ones are.
- o Sugar to attract, strengthen, and replicate the properties of the neighboring ingredients.

o (These ingredients can also be added to baked goods or desserts for the same effects, except more potent due to more energy spent while making and/or baking.)

# Going My Way

There is no need to dread Mondays anymore. A magical dish made with one or more of these combinations will assure a week of smooth sailing. Use this base combination the day ahead of a new week. Traditionally this meant a Sunday lunch or dinner.

### Base Combination

These base ingredients go well with any meat, fish, pork, poultry, and potato dish.

- o 1 part basil to attract wealth and help banish fears.
- o 1 part sage for wisdom and luck.
- o 1 part thyme to stay grounded and calm in the face of uncertainty.
- o 1 part oregano to promote good fortune.

### Herbed Butter

Use herbed butter during the cooking process, or enjoy with fresh breads or crackers.

If you don't make your own butter, you can always try purchasing a brick and simply adding the herbs. Try purchasing from a local farmer or farmers market, but store bought will do just fine as long as it is high quality.

If you do decide to buy your butter, place the purchased item inside a container marked with the Alchemist key and your intention (Vitality), and be mindful of it for at least day or two before adding herbs.

Add the following to the Base Combination listed above:

- o Butter for vitality, to encourage good things, and to encourage goodness from within.

### Rub for Roasted Chicken

Add the following to the Base Combination listed above:
- o 1 part salt to guard against negative vibrations and for an increase of positivity.
- o Chicken or chicken pieces, to provide a barrier against emotional attacks and negative thinking.

### Carrot Side Dish

Add the following to the Base Combination listed above:
- o 1 part salt to guard against negative vibrations and for an increase of positivity.
- o Carrots for energy and willpower.

### Beef Dish

Add the following to the Base Combination listed above:
- o 1 part salt to guard against negative vibrations and for an increase of positivity.
- o Beef (cuts or minced) to lessen feelings of aggression, and to encourage feelings of bliss and excitement.

## Love Boat

The old saying of winning a lover by winning their stomach first is very apt in this case. Do remember that love cannot grow from nothing. Yet, just as tiny seeds grow into the tallest of trees, this Base Combination and its variations can encourage the smallest flicker of love to grow into something with potential greatness.

Sometimes because of time or external influences, the fire of love**Error! Bookmark not defined.** dulls. This Base Combination and its variants are a great way to revive existing love.

## Base Combination

This list of base ingredients is perfect for fragrant turmeric rice, roasted chicken, or baked goods.

- o 1 part cardamon to increase sexual desire, and strengthen the existing bonds of love.
- o 1 part cloves so that you never feel lonely.

## Sweet Breads and Pumpkin Pies

Use in combination with your favorite pumpkin pie, sweet bread, or biscuit recipe. Though this does make for an interesting meat rub for pork.

- o Add the following to the Base Combination listed above:
- o 1 part cinnamon to warm hearts.
- o 1 part nutmeg to attract love.

## Fish Dish

Add the following to the Base Combination listed above:

- o 1 part black cumin to increase and strengthen the bonds of love.
- o Fish is used to encourage fertility, love, and lust.
- o Juice of a freshly squeezed lemon, or sliced lemon to enhance elements the magic in the dish.

### Savory Stew or Curry

Add some potato and keep it vegetarian, or add beef.

Add the following to the base ingredients listed above:

- o 1 part black cumin to increase and strengthen the bonds of love.
- o Kidney beans for love.

### Apple Desserts, Ciders, and Sauces

Add the following to the Base Combination listed above:

- o Red apples for attraction (Different recipes call for different apples, always check color and variation).
- o 1 part cinnamon to warm hearts.
- o 1 part nutmeg to attract love.
- o 1 vanilla bean for its hypnotic effect.

# Lustful Combinations

Whether it is something new, something you are hoping to happen, or even if you are already in a committed relationship and looking to spice things up, the following combinations can get those feelings of lust churning. However, lust is not the most important part about new feelings and new relationships, these examples below are only meant for side dishes and desserts. Use some, or all of them, with any of the combinations mentioned under the *Love Boat* section above.

### Sexy Salad

This salad goes well with the fish dish above and works best during summer months; or instead of a salad, turn them into fruit kebabs that make a pretty and delicious starter or dessert.

The Encyclopedia of Kitchen Witchery • 53

- Cucumber for calmness, rejuvenation, lust, and to throw a dash of glamour over the meal, making everything seem just a little more incredible than what it already is.
- Red Grapes to increase the psychic bond, and for lust.
- Sliced pear, soft variety and not crisp, to diminish mental blocks.
- Red Apples to attract and encourage love.
- Strawberries to increase feelings of love, and for luck.
- Cubed Honeydews to encourage love.
- Cubed oranges to replenish any needed motivation, passion or creativity.
- Fresh orange juice for dressing.

### Sultry Side Dish

- Sweet baby carrots to increase lust and energy.
- Sweet peas to encourage lustful feelings based on appearance.
- Chopped up fresh mint to enhance or stimulate the creation of a psychic connection between you and your partner.

### A Kiss of Dessert

Include the following as ingredients in a baked dessert, or simply use them to make rich and warm cocoa.

- Cocoa powder to stir feelings of love and compassion.
- Milk or cream for vitality and to encourage good things.
- Sweet pitted cherries for happiness and love.
- A sprinkle of fine chili pepper powder for a little spice in the bedroom.

### Strawberry Kisses

If you want to skip a heavy or warm dessert, this is the treat for you.

- o Strawberries to increase feelings of love.
- o Sugar to attract a kiss, and to strengthen neighboring ingredients.
- o Ice-cold water that will take on the qualities of neighboring ingredients.

Place strawberries in a flat dish, cover a quarter of the way with water, and sprinkle generously with sugar. Do this before you start cooking the main meal and refrigerate for at least one hour. Allow to stand at room temperature for thirty minutes, at which time you may add more sugar if you desire. Serve with cream.

## Coven Connection

Whether you are introducing a new member, are newly formed, or are a close-knit group with years of experience, the Coven Connection combinations are a wonderful way to bond.

You will find the ingredients are divided into three: A combination for a main dish, a secondary side dish, and a sweet treat. A meal made with one or more of these combinations works best when everyone gets involved, and goes well with the Psychic Link water combination (pg 61). And why not, as a group, try creating a secondary or side dish to add to it?

The meal, from cooking to eating to cleaning, is a form of bonding ritual. A way for your spiritual energies to connect, and at the same time stimulating and increasing the collective mana of the coven.

### Sea You

- o Fish (any white fish will work, flavor wise) to increase psychic powers, awareness, and psychic connection between the members.

o   Ginger for spiritual healing and for protection.
o   Scallions for communication and understanding.
o   Purple onion to increase power.

### Side With You

o   Potatoes to solidify and strengthen the magic within the meal.
o   Salt to protect against negative vibrations, allowing for positivity and more powerful magic.
o   Marjoram to solidify friendships and the coven.

### Sweet Connections

o   Cream to increase goodness.
o   Cherries for friendship.
o   Mango for an emotional and magical connection.
o   Pineapples to bestow luck (Remember to let everyone be involved in preparing the pineapple —even if it is just a single slice of the blade —while casting thoughts and infusing their mana into the pineapple. This will make sure everyone gets luck).
o   Mandarin for cheerfulness and friendship.

## Magic Magnifier

Our health and the things that happen in our day-to-day lives have an effect on, and drain, our mana. This can leave empaths feeling drained, cause readings to be a little muggy or inaccurate, make dream magic unstable, and be the reason for difficulties with graveyard walking, or communing with ghosts and spirits. You might even find your casting and the outcomes to be lacking.

If you don't have time to take a decent break and reinvigorate yourself, then this Magic Magnifier combination can be turned into a dish that is a magical holiday for the soul.

*(If you are a vegan or vegetarian, feel free to leave the beef out of the combination.)*

- o Beef to encourage bliss, also to increase spiritual protection and increases levels of mana.
- o Potatoes to strengthen the magic within the meal.
- o Purple onions for an increase in power.
- o Allspice to increase determination and increase levels and flow of mana.
- o Thyme for grounding, and to deepen the connection with nature.
- o Cilantro to deepen the connection to earth and nature.
- o Bay leaves for manifestation.
- o Butterbeans to sooth the spirit and attract less stress.
- o Salt to cleanse and protect your mana from negative vibrations.
- o Pepper to promote courage.

# Festive Feasting

Many of us take playing hostess very seriously. When you want your guests to leave with smiles and wanting more, then the Festive Feast combination makes for a fun event.

## Plateful of Party

If you don't eat pork, chicken will still work flavor wise. Or you can use the remaining ingredients in shortbreads or tarts.

- o Pork for a little chaos energy and to take on the magical properties of neighboring ingredients.
- o Sprigs of lemon balm to calm busy minds and spirits, and to bring out the happiness in each guest.
- o Apricots for rejuvenation.
- o Basil to dispel confusion and fears.

### Merry Mix

This combination will be great in a baked dessert, cakes and cookies, hot chocolate, or for ice-cream covered in warm chocolate sauce topped with cherries.

- o Milk, cream, or home-made ice-cream, for goodness and remembrance
- o Cocoa for compassion, love and acceptance of self as well as others.
- o Cinnamon for warm hearts and cool tempers.
- o Cayenne Pepper for light-hearted fun.
- o Cherries for friendship.

# Just Vibing

Negative energies can come from direct and indirect attacks. Direct attacks include the Evil Eye, curses, interactions with spirits and ghosts. Indirect attacks can unintentionally come from people with bad energy, or from those who sap energy from others.

Empaths tend to act like a magnet, attracting bad energy. Even those with shields and experience are susceptible to negative energy, especially during times of war and disaster.

It also comes from eating poorly, negative thinking, illness, smoking, pollution, and dehydration.

Some of the symptoms include lethargy, being exhausted both mentally and physically, depression, anxiety, and chronic worry. Magical symptoms can include psychic blocks, unable to astral travel or dream walk, as well as inconsistent readings and visions.

Here is a combination that can help replenish your energy, attract positive vibrations, bring calm, and help stabilize your mood.

**TIP:** To get the full effect, enjoy a round of meditation after eating, preferably outside. Sit on the grass, the dirt, or even a rock. Place the palms of your hands flat on the earth, and feel the bond grow and the energy pass through your hands and into you. Any buzzing you may feel in the palm of your hand is quite normal.

Ingredients:
- o Chicken for healing, protection, and spiritual grounding.
- o Black pepper for courage, to repel negative energy, and banish any curses.
- o Salt to cleanse, dispel negative energy and to protect your mana, for positivity, and to increase the magic infused within the meal as a whole.
- o Oregano to promote good will.
- o Button mushrooms for clarity.
- o Shiitake mushrooms for joy, pride, and satisfaction in who you are.
- o Maitake mushrooms to deepen your connection to the earth and nature.
- o Potatoes to strengthen the neighboring ingredients.

## Water Combinations

Under the section for water, we explain how important water is, to keep us hydrated as well as for healing, energy, and a sense of wellbeing. Not to mention how it connects us to universal life-force. Due to its importance, this book includes a list of tasty and magical water combinations for you to try.

Start the day with creating a magical blend, or potion if you will. Put a lot of thought when slicing your fruit, and for a visual extra, you can freeze blossoms, sprigs of mint, cherries, or strawberries and use these instead of regular ice blocks.

**TIP:** Boiled water will create clear ice cubes, whereas tap water will have varying shades of opaqueness.

Here are a few combinations to get you started. Sip throughout the day and enjoy the magic and taste.

**TIP:** Most of these combinations work well in a punch bowl, or when added to flavor lemonade.

### Zest Ahead

If you are expecting a long and busy day, this will help you get through it.

- Green apple for prosperity.
- Lemon for longevity.
- Carrot for energy and willpower.
- Orange for passion and creativeness.

### People Pleaser

If you are in a flirtatious mood, or just want to improve your connection with people you meet and interact with throughout the day, this combination will draw people to you and improve your likability.

- Sprigs of mint to encourage an emotional connection with everyone you interact with or meet.
- Strawberries to increase feelings of love within yourself and from those who interact with you.
- Blueberries to brighten and strengthen your aura.
- Raspberries to encourage kindness.

### Be Our Guest

Hosting a barbeque or summer luncheon? Then this combo will make sure that everyone has a good time.

- Orange for passion.
- Mandarin for cheerfulness, and friendship.
- Lemon for love.

## Drop of Luck

This is another one for when you are playing host. Serve this drink to your guests to encourage luck, love and prosperity. Due to the main ingredient being pineapple, you may partake but you might not be blessed the same way everyone else is. Not that we always need to be rewarded for good things!

- o Strawberry for luck and love.
- o Pineapple for luck and prosperity.
- o Cherries to attract happiness and love.

## Happy Day

Work hard, play hard, they say. That is sometimes easier said than done, though. So, in our busy lives we often make plans on what we will do with our spare time, and do not always have the energy to go through with it. This little pick-me-up is a great way to start your weekend, vacation, or even a day off from work.

- o Peaches for happiness and longevity.
- o Plums for spontaneity.
- o Spearmint to tackle self-doubt.
- o Apricots for rejuvenation.
- o Cherries for new friendships, or to strengthen old ones.

## Forgiveness

Sometimes things get out of hand and culminate in arguments. If you need help clearing the air afterward, this forgiveness blend is the best way to start.

- o Cinnamon sticks to cool tempers and help us remember the love that is there.
- o Firm pears (Red pears work best) for wisdom.
- o Pink apples to encourage a relaxed atmosphere.

## A Lusty Affair

Wanting to put a little spark back into your sex life? Whether you are looking for an interlude, or in a committed relationship that needs a bedroom boost, this combination will help get the electricity flowing.

- Kiwi to awaken sexual desires and make you sexually desirable.
- Oranges for passion.
- Red grapes to attract and increase the level of lust.

## Beautify

This combination is a quick and easy beauty spell, perfect for when you have a date or event coming up and need to look your ravishing best. Sip throughout the day between sunrise and sunset.

- Watermelon for beauty.
- Lychee for sweetness and beauty.
- Primrose flowers for beauty, youth, and to enhance the magic of the elixir and lengthen the time it works.

## Psychic Link

Whether you are new or experienced, this is a combo for those participating in things like graveyard walks, séances, readings, communing with spirits whether they may be human, demon, or the nature variety.

- Elderberry for psychic protection.
- Dandelion flowers to stimulate your natural psychic ability.
- Honeysuckle to give you the sight to see ghosts and spirits.
- Fresh cannabis leaves to increase psychic awareness.
- Fresh hemp leaves to protect you against psychic attacks.

### Third Eye Opener

The third eye is linked to perception, awareness, and communication with those on different planes of existence. If your third eye is blocked, your psychic vision a little weak, unclear or unreliable, or if you are just starting out and still learning how to control them, then this combination can help clear things up for you.

- o Sweet carrots to increase psychic awareness and visions.
- o Mint to stimulate psychic development.
- o Celery to boost or unlock natural psychic abilities.
- o Costmary to awaken your psychic sense.

### Cupid's Concoction

We don't have a bow and quiver filled with magical arrows, but with the help of this concoction you will be sending out all the right signals for love to come and find you.

- o Orange slices with rind, to attract love
- o Cloves (which can be stuck into the rind) to drive away loneliness.
- o 1 stick of cinnamon to draw people in.
- o Red apple slices to bring love.

## Fresh Fruit Teas

Fresh fruit teas are relatively easy to make, and whether you like it warm while winding down on a winter's evening, or ice cold while relaxing alongside the pool, they make for a delightful beverage.

Ingredients:

- o One tea bag (For grounding and soothing).
- o ¼ cup of freshly cut fruit pieces.

The Encyclopedia of Kitchen Witchery • 63

o   900 ml fire boiled water.

Instructions
1. Place tea bag and fruit into a jug.
2. Add water.
3. Steep for three minutes before removing tea bag.
4. Steep fruit for a further 10 minutes before straining.
5. Serve warm or leave to cool.
6. Add honey or sugar to flavor.

### Fruity Black Tea

Black Tea works well with the following fruits and combinations thereof:
o   Pineapple to bestow luck
o   Papaya to attract knowledge.
o   Peaches for happiness
o   Lemon for longevity.

### Fruity Green Tea

Green Tea works well with the following fruits and combinations thereof:
o   Cantaloupe to attract goodness.
o   Raspberries for kindness.
o   Blueberries to brighten auras.
o   Watermelon for beauty.

### Fruity Chamomile Tea

Chamomile Tea works well with the following fruits and combinations thereof:
o   Green Apples for prosperity.
o   Pink apples to improve and strengthen relationships.
o   Mango to stimulate loving feelings.

o  Orange for passion.

### Fruity Rooibos Tea

Rooibos Tea works well with the following fruits and combinations thereof:
o  Strawberries to attract luck.
o  Pineapple for prosperity.
o  Vanilla beans for good dreams.
o  Apricots for rejuvenation.

### Fruity White Tea

White Tea works well with the following fruits and combinations thereof:
o  Pear for wisdom.
o  Muskmelon to aid in manifestation.
o  Purple grapes to increase physic abilities.
o  Red grapes to increase feelings of lust.

### Fruity Oolong Tea

Oolong Tea works well with the following fruits and combinations thereof:
o  Cherries to attract happiness.
o  Plums to increase spontaneity.
o  Gooseberries to call for adventure.
o  Grapefruit to boost self-esteem.

# Shelved Magic and Magical Gifts

This chapter contains an array of ideas for shelved and magical gifts.

Anything made with magical intent and stored away for later use is referred to as shelved magic. Most of these items can also be used as magical gifts. This comes in handy when you feel someone is in need of a little kitchen witchery in their lives, but making them a meal is not an option.

Magical gifts (as with cooking) don't only work for those who practice magic, so you can still gift them to friends not within your circle. While you do not need to tell them about the magical side of the gift, it does tend to work better if you do. The reason being is that magical gifts become more powerful when accepted with gratitude, an open heart, and open mind. For whatever reason you do not want the receiver to know of the magical intent behind the gift, no need to worry. They are still as powerful as the magic infused within them.

Magical gifts can be shelved gifts, but they can also be more freshly made items like baked goods and butters.

Baked goods, bottled fruits, jams, and glazes all make wonderful magical gifts, whether you need a last-minute gift and still have some magically infused goods stored in the pantry, or are making it from scratch.

But not all shelved or magical gifts can be made in bulk and stored for time on end. Some have a lifespan as short as a week. Items such as cakes, cookies, and oils are usually best made as the need arises.

These ideas also work for gifts that contain more health-related benefits, the same process and magic goes into making them.

**TIP:** Place the Alchemist Key symbol somewhere on the container, even if as a label, or printed on decent cardboard or paper to hang around the neck of the bottle with natural string or twine. This will ensure the magic remains, and in some cases strengthens over time, till the gift has been consumed or used up. This can have bonus added effects: The more energy, creativity, and thought that goes into it, the more of your own mana is added.

**TIP:** While you are labeling things, remember to list your ingredients, the magical intention, date made, and expiry date when applicable.

## **Dried Fruit**

Long lasting and a good way to make sure that excess fruit does not go to waste, dried fruit is a delightful snack. If you do not have a food dehydrator, an oven will do just fine. You will find that some dry better than others. Home-made dried fruits can be stored for up to one year if sealed and stored properly.

Instructions:
1. Preheat your oven to 200 degrees Fahrenheit or 65 degrees Celsius.
2. Rinse ripe fruit and pat dry.
3. Trim away stems or leaves.
4. Cut fruit into thin slices.

5. Arrange the fruit for drying in a single layer on a baking sheet covered with parchment paper.
6. Dry your fruit for four to eight hours, depending on the size and water content of chosen fruit.
7. Check progress periodically. You will know when your dried fruit is ready by its slightly shriveled texture and chewiness.
8. Store your dried fruit in an airtight container, or a glass mason jar, at room temperature.

## Herbal Cooking Oil

**NOTE:** Fresh herbs can be used, but they must be wilted for a few hours beforehand. If the fresh herbs are not properly dried, the moisture within them may cause bacteria to grow in the oil. This is not safe. If you insist on using fresh herbs, the oil must be kept in the refrigerator and used within three to four days.

To err on the side of caution, we advise using dry herbs instead: One or two tablespoons to one cup of oil. Bruise the herbs with a rolling pin or a pestle and mortar beforehand to release the flavors.

The best oils to use would be high quality almond, coconut, sunflower, avocado, and olive oil. Remember to get the flavorless variety when it comes to coconut. Pair infused olive oil with fresh bread for a treat on the taste buds and sense of smell. Each oil and combination of herbs will have its own lifespan ranging from one year to five years. Do your research and remember the rule: If it smells off, it usually is.

Once you have mixed your dry herb into the oil of your choice, mix and store in sterilized airtight bottles. Label and store in a dark cool place for several weeks before using. The longer the herbs have been steeping in the oil, the more fragrant and flavorful the oils become.

# **Flavored Extracts**

Most store-bought extracts are completely artificial. By making your own flavored extracts, you can infuse them with magic intention, and shelve them. All you need is high quality vodka that is not less than 40 percent alcohol. Because you use so little at a time, we recommend infusing them with only one magical intention.

To get you started, below you will find a list of ideas. Some are sweet, usually used in baking. Some are savory, usually used when you want a stronger aroma in a meal, especially if you are using fresh herbs that lose much of their aroma while cooking.

**TIP:** Storing in a bottle with a dropper/ piquette makes for easier use.

Add any of the following to one cup of vodka:
- o Sweet Dream - 6 Vanilla bean pods.
- o Love - ½ cup raw and unsalted crushed almonds.
- o Longevity - Rinds of two lemons.
- o Creativity - Rinds of one orange.
- o Love and romance - Rinds of one lemon and ½ an orange.
- o Cleansing - 1 cup of mint leaves.
- o Depression -1 cup of spearmint leaves.
- o Protection - ¼ to ½ cup of shredded ginger.
- o Calm - ½ cup of freshly shredded coconut.
- o Cool tempers - 4 sticks of cinnamon.
- o Detach negative energy - ¼ cup of decarbed hemp leaves.
- o Chakra activation - ¼ cup of decarbed cannabis leaves.
- o For clear thoughts and to remember the good times - ¼ cup of basil and ¼ cup of rosemary.
- o For passionate sex - ¼ to ½ cup dried chili peppers of your choice, feel free to mix a variety.

The Encyclopedia of Kitchen Witchery • 71

o Grounding and longevity - ¼ cup Thyme and rind of ½ lemon.
o For victory - ½ cup Sweet woodruff.

Gently shake the bottle or container for a few minutes. Store in a dark cool place. Store for about two weeks before using. Use a teaspoonful at a time, add more if you feel you need more aroma and a little extra magic.

## Vodka Combinations

Vodka is not only for extracts.

- Vodka that is 40 percent alcohol content can be infused and added to cocktails, punch bowls, or just diluted with lemonade and ice.
- For cocktail syrups, vodka of 50 percent and higher is needed for better flavor extraction.
- For liqueurs, dilute infused vodka with a simple sugar syrup.

Remember to wash and pat fruit dry before cutting and preparing. A good ratio is one cup of fruit to two cups of vodka, and leave to infuse for three to five days before straining and removing fruit. This fruit is a great treat when added to ice-cream. Here are a few fun combinations you can try:

o Love - Strawberries and basil.
o Togetherness and to release inhibitions - Cranberries and lime.
o Brighten auras and encourage kindness - Blueberries and raspberries.
o Wish granting and luck - Pomegranate and strawberries.
o For calmed thoughts and happiness - Coconut and lychees.
o Cheer, passion, and abundance - Mandarin, nutmeg, and star anise.
o Motivation, knowledge, and success - Papaya, orange and kiwi.

- o Happiness and longevity - Peaches and apricots.
- o Love and sex - Kiwi and strawberries.
- o For reinvigoration, manifestation, and gratitude - Watermelon, muskmelon, and cantaloupe.

## Sweet Syrups

Simply based on taste, you might never buy store made syrups again, but these magical syrups are perfect for pancakes, flapjacks, crumpets, and ice-cream or to brush over freshly made cake to preserve the moisture.

**NOTE**: Store in a glass jar, or bottle, in the refrigerator for up to one month.

**TIP**: Some of the examples below contain herbs and flowers, and to some, the texture can detract from the experience. In these instances, place the ingredients in filter bags or tea bags.

- o 1 cup brown sugar.
- o 1 cup of water.
- o Fruit.

Instructions:

Add water and sugar and other chosen ingredients to the pot over medium heat, stirring until sugar dissolves. Focus on the sugar and how it will amplify and take on the magical properties of any ingredient paired with it. Set aside until cool.

Here is a list of combinations ideas to flavor the simple syrup mixture.

- o Longevity, creativity, and happiness - ¼ to ½ cup Mandarin, orange, and lemon (remove as much of the bitter white pith).
- o Love and fidelity - 1 tsp of basil and ½ cup strawberries.

The Encyclopedia of Kitchen Witchery • 73

- o Wisdom and prosperity - ¼ cup pear and ¼ cup green apple.
- o Love and lust - ¼ cup cucumber and ¼ cup red apple.
- o For healing, protection, and resolve - 1/2 cup blackberries, ½ cup blueberries, and ¼ cup elderberries.
- o Attract spiritual healing and sweet thoughts - 4 to 6 rooibos teabags and replace brown sugar with honey.
- o To quiet the mind - 4 bags of oolong, black, white, or green teabags.
- o Peace and passion - ½ cup hibiscus and ½ cup lavender.
- o Dream of love - ½ cup rose petals.
- o No more nightmares - ½ cup of chamomile and ¼ cup of catnip.
- o Busy days and sweet dreams - ¼ cup of coffee beans and ½ cup vanilla beans or pods.

# Fruit Puree

This is where a blender or food processor comes in handy. Fruit puree can be bottled and stored for two days in the refrigerator, or six months in the freezer. Not only is it a great way to give a baby a magical dish, but it can be used in a variety of ways: baked good, smoothies, milkshakes, cheesecakes; or added to yogurt, ice-cream, and cocktails; and even for meat toppings.

Here are a few ways to use your fruit puree in magical gifts.

**TIP:** If you have a favorite recipe in the baked goods division, exchange half the oil or butter for a quarter of the amount of fruit puree. Not only does this add magic to your recipe, but it cuts down the calories too.

### Fruit Cookies

This is a fun snack or gift for adults and kids alike, and you can experiment with putting dried pieces of fruit, or nuts, into the mix. Place a few in a mason jar and tie a ribbon around its neck for a yummy magical gift.

- o 3 tablespoons of fruit puree
- o 1 cup of butter (softened to room temp)
- o 1 ½ cups of sugar
- o 1 large egg
- o 2 ¾ cups of all-purpose flour
- o ½ tsp of baking powder
- o 1 tsp of extract (pair aroma with fruit choice, if in doubt use vanilla)
- o ½ tsp of salt

Instructions:

1. Preheat the oven to 350 degrees Fahrenheit or 175 degrees Celsius.
2. Grease baking sheet.
3. Cream the butter and the sugar until fluffy.
4. Add egg and puree, mix thoroughly.
5. Add the flour, baking powder, salt, and vanilla essence, and fold until the flour is fully incorporated.
6. Roll teaspoon sized scoops of dough into balls, and place 1 ½ inches apart and flatten lightly with thumb or spoon.
7. Bake for 10-15 minutes until lightly browned. Leave to cool on the baking tray for five minutes before transferring them to a cooling rack.

### Fruit Muffins

These muffins can be enjoyed anytime of the day. Take them with on picnics and road trips, or as a magical gift to a hostess or friend. They definitely stand out!

- o 2/3 cup of fruit puree
- o 2/3 cup of plain flour
- o 1 ½ teaspoon baking powder
- o 100 ml milk

The Encyclopedia of Kitchen Witchery • 75

- o 1 egg
- o Optional ¼ cup of raisons/chopped fruit/dry fruit/ chocolate chips
- o Optional pinch of cinnamon/nutmeg

Instructions:

1. Preheat oven to 375 degrees Fahrenheit or 190 degrees Celsius and grease muffin tins.
2. Mix everything together and fill muffin tin to ¾ full.
3. Bake for 30-40 minutes or until tester comes out clean.

### Fruit Cake

Let your cake stand above the everyday vanilla and chocolate. Use can even use the same fruit or puree to decorate this fruity delight.

- o 1 cup fruit puree
- o 2 1/4 cups cake flour
- o 1 1/2 teaspoon baking powder
- o 3/4 teaspoon baking soda
- o ½ teaspoon salt
- o 3 eggs
- o 1 1/2 cups sugar
- o 1 1/2 cups butter
- o 1 teaspoon extract (pair aroma with fruit choice, if in doubt use vanilla)

Instructions:

1. Preheat the oven to 350 degrees Fahrenheit or 175 degrees Celsius.
2. Grease baking pan(s).
3. Mix the cake flour, baking powder, baking soda, and salt together in a large bowl.

4. In a separate bowl, whisk the eggs before adding, sugar, fruit puree, butter, and extract.
5. Add the wet ingredients to the dry ingredients and combine until incorporated.
6. Poor into pan(s) and bake for 40 to 45 minutes, or until tester comes out clean, rotating pan 180 degrees halfway through.
7. Transfer to rack and allow to cool.

### Fruit Mousse

- ¾ cup fruit puree
- 2 cups heavy whipping cream
- 7 ounces sweetened condensed milk

Instructions
1. Whip the whipping cream and sweetened condensed milk until soft peaks form.
2. Fold in fruit puree and blend gently until puree is fully incorporated.
3. Spoon into a large serving bowl or individual ramekins, cover with plastic wrap and chill till set.

### Citrus Pudding

This delightful pudding can be served either hot or cold, and pairs well with ice-cream and custard. This recipe can be made with grapefruit, oranges, lemon, or mandarin. If you are feeling adventurous, feel free to mix and match!

Ingredients for base:
- 1 cup fruit juice
- ½ cup chopped up fruit
- 1 tablespoon grated zest
- 2/3 cup soft butter

The Encyclopedia of Kitchen Witchery • 77

- o 1 ¾ cups white sugar
- o 2 teaspoons fruit extract (pair aroma with fruit choice, if in doubt use vanilla)
- o 3 cups of flour
- o 2 ½ teaspoons baking powder

Instructions:
1. Preheat oven to 350 degrees Fahrenheit or 180 degrees Celsius.
2. Grease oven-proof glass bowl.
3. Sift together dry ingredients and put aside.
4. In a large bowl cream butter and sugar until light and fluffy.
5. Add eggs one at a time, then vanilla, then zest.
6. Mix in half the dry ingredients, then half the juice, followed by the remaining flour, and then the remaining juice.
7. Pour into greased oven-proof bowl(s), bake for 25 to 30 minutes, or until tester comes out clean. While it is baking, make the sauce.

Sauce: Bring ingredients to a simmer until the sugar is melted. If sweet enough, remove from heat. Else, proceed to add more sugar.

Once the cake base has been removed from the oven, poke holes into the top of it, using something like a chopstick or the back of a thin wooden spoon.

Gently pour over Citrus Sauce and allow five minutes to cool before eating as a warm winter dessert, or place in fridge to cool completely for a light summer dessert.

## Jams

The ratio of fruit to sugar is 1:1 when making jam. This recipe works best with berries and pitted fruit.

Always sterilize jars and discard any lids that show signs of rust. Place jars in an oven heated to 250 degrees Fahrenheit or 120 degrees Celsius for 15 minutes. After which you must keep them in the oven at the lowest heat possible until needed. Prepare seals by soaking them in boiling water until flexible. The seals must have a plastic lining on the inside.

Ingredients
- o 2 lb. or 900 grams fresh fruit that has been washed peeled, seeded, pitted, and chopped up.
- o 2 lb. or 900 grams white sugar
- o ½ lemon

Instructions:
1. Place prepared fruit in a large stainless-steel pot or saucepan, cover with sugar.
2. Squeeze the lemon juice into the fruit mixture, slice and add whatever remains of the lemon, and stir until combined.
3. Let the mixture sit at room temperature for three hours so that the sugar can draw out some of the natural juices.
4. Place over medium heat and bring to boil.
5. Stir often to prevent the mixture from bubbling over.
6. To test if the jam is ready, take a small spoonful and drop it onto a small, cold plate. It should be more of a dollop than droplets, or the consistency of the drop must become thick after it cools.
7. Ladle into prepared, sterilized, and still hot jam jars, leaving 1/8 inch space between the jam and the lid.

**WARNING:** If you spoon hot jam into a cold bottle, it will shatter.

Wipe edges, close tightly, turn upside down and leave to cool. Store in a refrigerator.

**NOTE:** The upside-down method is not favored by food safety professionals. This is a very outdated technique and was replaced by the 'Boiling water bath' method. That said, many jam makers still recommend the upside-down method.

**TIP:** If you prefer your jam less sweet, sugar can be reduced to 450 grams. Jam lasts up to one month when refrigerated.

Popular (combination) choices are:
- Rejuvenation - Apricot
- Determination and happiness - Blueberry and cherry
- Courage and luck - Strawberry and one teaspoon crushed black pepper, whole black pepper corns to be added before bottling, for visual effect.
- Wisdom and fair relationships - Pears and pink apples
- Love and sex - Kiwi and strawberry
- Luck and kindness - Raspberry and pomegranate
- Beauty and prosperity - Plum and green apple
- Adventure and love - Gooseberries and crisp red apples
- Determination and to lessen inhibitions - Blueberries and lime
- Spirit talks and graveyard walks (Perfect for Halloween) - Pumpkin and ginger

### Chocolate

Whether as a gift to someone else or yourself, chocolate is always a winner.

Ingredients:
- 2 cups cocoa powder
- 1/2 cup fine white sugar
- 1/4 teaspoon flour

- o 3/4 cup butter
- o 2/3 cup milk
- o 1 cup Water

Instructions:

1. Mix the cocoa and the butter until a paste is formed.
2. Add the sugar, flour, and milk and mix until smooth.
3. Heat a pan and fill it about 1/4 full with water. Place the bowl with the cocoa mixture in the water.
4. On a low to medium heat, whisk the mixture until it is warm all the way through and remove from heat.
5. Add the sugar, flour, and milk mixture to the cocoa paste. Mix thoroughly and continuously until the batter is lump free and smooth.
6. Pour the mixture in the molds and refrigerate.

This recipe can work as a base for your own creation. Add nuts, raisins, dried fruits, chili, sea salt, mint, spear mint, and whatever else you can think of! Wrap neatly in tinfoil or arrange in an airtight container.

## DRIED FRUIT TEAS

Besides the health benefits and the amazing taste, fruit teas made from dry fruits, leaves, and spices are hydrating and can easily replace hot caffeinated beverages as well as cold fizzy drinks. It's as easy as chopping up your dried fruit.

Purchase some filter bags or empty tea bags and create your own favorite magical mixes that you can store away for a rainy day or use as a magical gift. For now, here are a few of our favorites:

- o Upliftment, motivation, kindness, and a bright future - Rose, orange, raspberry, and green apple.
- o Lessen self-doubt and increase self-love - Spearmint and strawberry.

The Encyclopedia of Kitchen Witchery • 81

- o Fertility, sexual desire, and magnetism - Pomegranate, cardamon, and cinnamon.
- o To warm the heart, stir peace, and gift luck - Ginger, figs, and pineapple (Serve to group. See Pineapple.).
- o Happiness and longevity - Apricots and peaches.
- o Psychic awakening and feminine magic - Anise and fig.
- o For luck in love - Strawberry and mango.
- o For feminine charm and love - Mango and vanilla.
- o Friendship, passion, and togetherness - Cherries, orange, and cranberries.
- o To brighten an aura and increase kindness, wisdom, and love - Blueberry, raspberry, pear, and strawberry.
- o Luck, popularity, and cheerfulness - Apples, mandarin, and strawberries.

## Herbed Butter

On fresh bread, crackers, toast, or potatoes, herbed butter is an easy way to brighten up the taste on these old favorites. You can make your own butter or use soft high quality salted, or unsalted, butter. Unsalted butter will need salt added.

Use a mold or a butter stamp to personalize your bricks.

- o Fearlessness, good fortune, and repel bad luck - Basil, oregano, and chives
- o Repel negative energy and spirits, and replenish and restore damaged mana- Tarragon and parsley
- o To cleanse and connect with nature - Garlic and thyme
- o Psychic development and to dispel fears - Mint and basil
- o Hope and wisdom - Oregano and sage
- o Lessen the sadness of old memories and for a peaceful life - Rosemary and lavender
- o Protection from all negative energies - Parsley and chives
- o Divination and spirit talking/graveyard walking - Chives and horseradish

- Hope, protection, and cleansing - Oregano, parsley, and garlic
- Find balance and beauty - Dill and lemon rind.
- Courage and connecting nature - Black pepper and cilantro

# Vinaigrettes

Vinaigrettes can be used in place of a salad dressing, or to marinade meat, or baste vegetables. Do not shy away from adding ¼ cup of chopped fruits like grapes or any of the berries.

Ingredients
- 1 cup of oil
- ½ cup of acids
- 3 Tablespoons flavor
- Whisk your ingredients together and store in an airtight bottle in the refrigerator for up to one week.

For oils use any of the following:
- Olive oil
- Avocado Oil
- Walnut Oil
- Sesame Seed Oil

For acids, use any of the following:
- Lemon juice
- Orange juice
- Vinegar

Flavor combos:
- For astral traveling and bonding with nature - Lavender and thyme.
- Solidify bond of coven/friendship, promote goodwill, and dispel fear - Marjoram, basil, and oregano.

The Encyclopedia of Kitchen Witchery • 83

- o Heighten sex drive, dispel jealousy, and protection from infidelity - Basil, black pepper, and ¼ cup fresh and finely chopped strawberries.
- o Increase bond and lust - ¼ cup celery and lovage.
- o Neutralize negative energy and aid psychic development - Dill and Mint.
- o Protection against graveyard spirits and deepen bond with the nature - Garlic and cilantro.
- o For better understanding of nature spirits, as well as deepen bond nature, and to attract good things - Fennel, cilantro, and black mustard seeds.
- o Ward off evil and nightmares, for cleansing and brightening aura - peppermint, catnip, parsley, and ¼ cup blueberries.

## Bottled Fruit

A perfect way to store away seasonal fruit. Most fruit can be bottled with a simple sugar syrup. Don't be shy to add a few leaves of your favorite herb or spice, like spearmint, cinnamon, or vanilla beans.

Always sterilize jars and discard any lids that show signs of rust. Place jars in an oven heated 250 degrees Fahrenheit or 120 degrees Celsius for 15 minutes. Keep them in the oven at the lowest heat possible until needed. Prepare seals by soaking them in boiling water till flexible. The seals must have a plastic lining on the inside.

Your ratio of sugar to water depends entirely on how tart or sweet your fruit is, or your sweetness preference:

- Light syrup - 3 cups water to ½ cup sugar
- Medium syrup - 3 cups water to 1 cup sugar
- Heavy syrup - 3 cups water to 2 cups sugar

Instructions:

1. Wash, dry, and prepare your fruit. Discard any bruised fruit.
2. Add water and sugar to a pot and boil until sugar has dissolved.
3. Fill prepared jars with fruit, and carefully add sugar syrup until the jar is full.
4. Wipe the rim and, using tongs, retrieve the hot lids from the boiling water and seal jars tightly.
5. Heat the oven to 275 degrees Fahrenheit or 140 degrees Celsius.
6. Place the full jars in a roasting pan in the oven for 50-60 minutes.
7. Carefully remove the jars from the oven, leave overnight before testing if the jars have sealed correctly (the lid will be slightly concave).
8. Store in a dark cool place for twelve to twenty-four months.

# Healthy Combinations

It's not always a magical benefit we seek, but a health-related one. Having a healthy balanced diet, especially one that includes variety, is a sure way to keep our physical and spiritual energy in peak form. It can also ease the pains and discomfort that come with sickness and ailments.

In this chapter, we give you a few options for on those days you could use the medicinal help of home cooking. Remember that this does not replace the need for a health care professional; and when symptoms don't ease or subside, it's best to go see one.

The following are combinations of foods that go well together in cooking, taste, and health. They are just basic combinations that you can pair with other ingredients for a main or side dish, but we have given you a few ideas on what dishes you could prepare.

### Migraine Mixes

If you suffer from regular bouts of migraines, cook and eat one of the following combinations 1 – 2 times per week

COMBO ONE
- Fatty fish like salmon
- Almonds

One way to use these ingredients is by crushing the almonds to make a crust for your fish.

COMBO TWO

- Avocado
- Almonds

Goes great as main ingredients to a salad, along with mandarin.

COMBO THREE
- Ginger
- Sweet woodruff

Create a non-alcoholic syrup, or create a ginger loaf and cookies with a twist.

COMBO FOUR
- Bay leaves
- Spinach

Turn into soup, or add finely chopped olives and bake into savory rolls for the dinner table.

## Cholesterol Buster

Your body needs a certain level of cholesterol to make cell membranes, hormones, and the very important vitamin D. Too much cholesterol can limit blood flow and result in a heart attack or a stroke.

If you are suffering from high cholesterol numbers, use any of the following combinations at mealtimes three to four times a week.

COMBO ONE
- Artichoke
- Oregano
- Kidney beans

This combination makes for tasty paella, salads, or stews.

COMBO TWO
- o Fatty fish like salmon
- o Peas
- o Paprika

Try adding honey for glaze with a sprig of saffron, or turn this into a cold dish or salad for hot summer days.

COMBO THREE
- o Apples
- o Almonds

Whether baked into squares and desserts, or as part of brilliant tasty stuffing for chicken or turkey, choose your apples accordingly.

COMBO FOUR
- o Strawberry
- o Walnut
- o Black pepper

This is another delicious combination for stuffing, or can be added to a salad.

## Inflammation

Inflammation is your body's way of protecting you from bacteria and help heal injuries. As with most things, there must be balance; too much inflammation can have negative effects, which include heat, redness, pain, and swelling.

Chronic inflammation comes with its own set of physical side-effects including extreme pain, fatigue, insomnia, constipation, diarrhea, acid reflux, weight loss, or weight gain. Not to mention the mental effects such as depression, anxiety, and mood disorders.

COMBO ONE
- o Lamb
- o Basil
- o Parsnips
- o Onions

It can be as simple as throwing them all together into a roasting pan or oven proof dish.

COMBO TWO
- o Anise seeds
- o Pears

Spiced pears are easy enough, but why not try your hand at a Bundt cake with this combination?

COMBO THREE
- o Celery
- o Leeks
- o Bay leaves

Braised, sautéed, or in a salad, this combination makes for quick and easy meal ideas.

COMBO FOUR
- o Tarragon
- o Cabbage

This combination is best used roasted or turned into slaw.

COMBO FIVE
- o Porcini mushrooms
- o Basil
- o Tarragon

Melt a little butter and fry in a pan, or do something more elaborate like a mushroom and potato dish with fresh cream and brown onion soup powder in the oven.

COMBO SIX
- o Pineapple
- o Yams

Roast them. Candy them. Get creative with baked desserts or use them in your pumpkin pie recipe. Feel free to leave out the actual pumpkin if you want.

COMBO SEVEN
- o Rhubarb
- o Cranberry
- o Elderberry

Perfect for spritzers, cocktails, jams, or baked goods, such as rhubarb with a berry twist crisp.

### Cancel Cancer

If only it were that easy, but there are things we can do to help our body fight cancer cells, help shrink tumors, and decrease our chances of getter the big and infamous 'C', and if you are eating five fruits and vegetables a day, you are halfway there!

Here are a few combinations that you can use two to three times a week if you are worried, or more if you have been diagnosed.

FOR EVERY MEAL OR COMBO
- o Cannabis and hemp.

Decarb and use the herb in any savory dish. Alternatively, you can infuse butter or coconut oil with it. Use the mixture in place of regular butter and oil. The butter makes for delicious tasting baked goods, especially when paired with chocolate, peanut butter, or vanilla.

BONUS: Once infused into coconut oil, you can use it for skin cancer by applying it directly to your skin. Scented coconut works better for this simply because you walk around smelling like a coconut cookie or pina colada for the remainder of the day.

COMBO ONE
- o Strawberry
- o Tea (Black, white, oolong, or green)

Sweeten with honey or add ice cubes to cool.

COMBO TWO
- o Cauliflower
- o Broccoli

A few spoonfuls of water, some salt, and pepper, and blanch these two in a pot together. If you are not a fan of these two, try adding some béchamel sauce. Or turn that béchamel sauce into a rich cheese sauce with a few handfuls of yellow cheese and a splash of more milk.

COMBO THREE

The Encyclopedia of Kitchen Witchery • 91

- o Chicken
- o Cloves
- o Lemon

Poke the cloves into the chicken, this makes them easier to find and remove before serving. Squeeze out the lemon juice and use the remains as stuffing with butter. Use the juice for basting and change it up by trying it with different combinations of orange juice, honey, and cinnamon.

COMBO FOUR
- o Enoki mushrooms
- o Garlic

Brush the mushrooms with butter garlic and wrap them in bacon, or fry them with noodles or butter.

COMBO FIVE
- o Porcini mushrooms
- o Oregano

These flavors go well with chicken, Italian sausage, steak or simply fried with butter.

COMBO SIX
- o Walnuts
- o Peaches

Any dish involving grilled or baked peaches and walnuts is a winner. For something lighter, simply add to salad.

COMBO SIX
- o Pomegranate

o Cranberry
o Persimmon

Add this combination to yogurt or your daily smoothie.

COMBO SEVEN
o Rhubarb
o Blueberry
o Gooseberries

This combination makes for excellent pies and tartlets with cream, or try your hand at chutney and jam.

COMBO EIGHT
o Lemon
o Ginger

Turn this combination into a cup of tea with honey to taste. This makes for a delightful cake that goes well with lemon syrup, icing, or filling.

**Brain Health**

It's important to stimulate your brain health on a daily basis. There are a few different ways you can do this:
o You can engage your brain; Sudoku, reading, puzzles, and creative outlets like writing and painting are perfect examples of ways to do this.
o Stay socially engaged. Spending time with friends and family is the easy option, but don't limit yourself. Attend

talk shows and book readings by yourself. Join a club and meet new people. Try new things.

o Manage stress with meditation techniques, healthy eating, and self-regulating your emotions.
o Exercise, even if it is just a short walk.
o Sleep. Take as much time and effort with your pre-sleep routine as you would for your morning or pre-date routine.
o And healthy eating!

Below are a few combinations that revolve especially around brain health. Aim to include one combination per week, or more if you have a genetic disposition for brain diseases.

COMBO ONE
o Pork
o Sweet potato/yam
o Rooibos
o Sugar

A personal favorite of mine is Rooibos tea with sweet potatoes:

Melt some butter, add sugar and honey, chopped up yams or sweet potatoes, and two or more cups of strong rooibos tea. Leave to boil until yams or sweet potatoes are done and falling apart. Mix a little custard powder with a little cold water, stir in and allow to thicken. Serve as a side dish with pork. This is even better when served with a spicy pork dish. Add extra honey at any stage, especially during the reheating of any leftovers.

COMBO TWO
o Broccoli
o Carrots
o Sage

Steam or roast with olive oil. Add a little lemon juice if desired.

COMBO THREE
- o Enoki mushroom
- o Egg

Make mushroom pancakes, scrambled eggs, or a quiche.

COMBO FOUR
- o Fish (Salmon, tuna, and herring would be the best options.)
- o Blackberries

Turn the blackberries into a glaze or vinaigrette that goes well with pan seared fish, or simply sprinkle them whole and fresh over your fish.

COMBO FIVE
- o Cocoa
- o Dates
- o Walnuts
- o Cashews

Create chocolate date balls or add to vanilla ice-cream.

COMBO SIX
- o Gooseberries
- o Apples

Create delicious tarts, pies, or crumbles with these two. Consider adding cinnamon, anise seed, and nutmeg to the mix.

COMBO SEVEN

- Fish/shellfish
- Tangerines

Turn your tangerines into a sauce or relish that is incredible with grilled fish. Or try adding tangerine juice to a pan of scallops while cooking.

### Gut Health

It's not all about physique. Gut health is about absorbing the energy and nutrients from foods we eat, clearing toxins, fighting against heart disease and inflammation. Poor gut health can influence your mood, or make you feel sluggish and tired. Worse, poor gut health can lead to diarrhea, constipation, gas, bloating, and abdominal pains. Here are a few combinations that you can eat to improve your gut health. Aim for these combinations one to three times per week, or more if you are currently experiencing the symptoms of poor gut health.

COMBO ONE
- Sweet potatoes
- Apples
- Pears

Add some maple for glaze and you have a delightful casserole to put in the oven or turn them into a fruit puree that can be used in baking. See Fruit puree recipes under the Chapter for Shelved and magical gifts.

COMBO TWO
- Bananas
- Dates
- Almonds

Turn this combination into a yummy smoothie or bake them into a banana date loaf.

COMBO THREE
- o Ginger
- o Chia seeds

Create smoothies, pudding, or teas.

COMBO FOUR
- o Lentils
- o Leeks
- o Oregano
- o Garlic
- o Onion

Add some potatoes and you have the beginnings of a fragrant vegan soup, or try butter beans instead for curry.

## Colds and Flu

It is difficult to enjoy the beauty of winter and rainy months when suffering with colds, flu, or similar symptoms. Here are a few combinations that will get you back on your feet in no time.

COMBO ONE
- o Chicken with the skin
- o Garlic
- o Broccoli
- o Lemon
- o Lemongrass

Chicken broth or soup is both comforting and healing.

COMBO TWO
- o  Cardamon
- o  Hibiscus
- o  Honey
- o  Ginger

Use these to create teas, or add cinnamon and nutmeg and get baking.

COMBO THREE
- o  Chicken
- o  Kumquats
- o  Oranges

Create a one pan dish with chicken, kumquat, and orange juice and rind. Or keep it simple and create a mini citrus side dish to go with your favorite chicken dish.

COMBO FOUR
- o  Mint
- o  Chili

Get creative with hot chocolate or ice-cream sauces.

COMBO FIVE
- o  Mint
- o  Chamomile

Tea is your easiest option with these two.

## COMBO SIX
- o Kiwi
- o Banana
- o Spinach

This makes for a filling and good tasting breakfast smoothie.

The Encyclopedia of Kitchen Witchery • 99

Cassandra Sage

# Part Three

# Herbs and Spices

### What is the difference between herbs and spices?

Herbs are the leafy part of a plant and can be used either fresh or dried. Spice can come from the root, bark, fruit, stem, seed, or flower of a tree or plant, and is always used after it has been dried.

Compared to herbs, spices tend to be stronger in flavor. Dried herbs have a deeper flavor than their fresh counterpart, meaning you require less dry herb than you would fresh herb (Ratio 1 to 3). Dried herbs can be added from the beginning, whereas fresh herbs should be used closer to the end in order to get the most out of the flavor.

To get the most flavor out of your dry herbs, gently bruise them with a rolling pin or with a pestle and mortar.

### Storing Herbs and Spices

Whether store-bought or homemade, herbs have a shelf life of one to three years. After which point the health and magical properties diminish and expire. Your telltale signs for expired herbs are usually loss of color, taste, and aroma.

Whole spices can be kept in an airtight container for up to four years. Ground spices on the other hand, only last six months to two years when stored in the same way. Once they have lost their smell, they no longer have health or magical benefits.

- ✿ Your best bet is placing the herbs and spices in airtight containers, bottles, or even zip lock bags.
- ✿ Labels are important, remember to include dates and the Alchemist Key to unlock and steadily increase the magical potential over time.

- Store in dark cool areas, out of direct sunlight, heat, and moisture.

Fresh herbs are a little trickier, but stored properly they can last two to three weeks.

- We start by washing the fresh herbs. Use a cold stream of water to gently rinse off debris. Set on paper towels and blot away the moisture and dry gently. Remove any wilted or browning leaves.
- Hardy herbs like thyme and sage should be placed side by side on slightly dampened clean paper towels. Roll them up the way you would a sushi roll. Place in a zip lock bag or wrap in cellophane before placing in the refrigerator.
- With regards to the softer herbs like mint and parsley, remove the majority of the stems and seal in a mason jar with a small bit of water and place in the refrigerator. Try standing them upright in the jar if possible.
- Fresh basil should be stored the same way as soft herbs, with the exception that it should remain at room temperature in a well-lit area, but out of direct sunlight. It can be stored this way for up to two weeks.
- Keep fresh ginger and turmeric in a bag pierced with holes for up to two weeks.
- Store garlic heads in a cool dark place, as close to the ground as possible. Garlic can be used until it starts showing sign of mold or starts growing sprouts.

## Herbs and Spices

A

**ALFALFA (Medicago Sativa)**

**AKA** Lucerne or Purple medic

Alfalfa has an earthy taste and can be added to omelets, salads, stews, soups, sauces, dips, hummus, pasta, casseroles, oatmeal, pancake batter, and smoothies.

**Magical Uses**

Add Alfalfa to your cooking if you wish to attract or increase prosperity in your life, it comes with the added side effect of it increasing thankfulness and appreciation for what you already have.

## Healing Qualities

Adding Alfalfa to your diet can aid in lowering cholesterol, and in relieving symptoms of menopause. It can decrease irritability and nervousness. When combined with peppermint in a smoothie or tea, it can soothe an irritable stomach.

## ALLSPICE (Pimenta Dioca)

**AKA** Jamaican Pepper or Pimento

Allspice has a powerful flavor and fragrance. A few berries will add a warmth and spiciness to any dish, but it pairs best with lamb and beef. Ground up, it can be sprinkled lightly over roasted vegetables. It's great for adding a peppery depth to stews, curries, and soups. Also, don't forget to pair it with sweet dishes such as gingerbread, apple pie, and dark chocolate desserts for that added zing.

## Magical Uses

Use allspice in your cooking if you are looking to attract money, luck, determination, and emotional healing. You can also add allspice to your food if you are looking to temporarily increase the strength of your magic.

## Healing Qualities

Allspice has anti-inflammatory and pain-relieving properties. It is also a great immune booster and promotes oral health.

## ANISE SEEDS (Pimpinella Anisum)

**AKA** Aniseed or Anix or Sweet Cumin

Anise seeds can be used whole or ground into a powder. Anise seeds have a sweet, fragrant aroma with a strong, licorice taste that is sweet and mildly spicy. Anise seed, whole or ground, can be added to dough for baked goods, fruit fillings for pies, and ground meat such as lamb or beef.

## Magical Uses

Use Anise seed in your cooking if you are looking to infuse some extra happiness into your life.

Add Anise seed to your food if you are looking to stimulate latent or underdeveloped psychic ability. If infused with this purpose, avoid giving to young children, even those showing natural psychic abilities and proclivity, for the pure reason that it can overstimulate.

Anise can also ward off evil intention, also known as the Evil Eye.

**Healing Qualities**

Anise seed helps calm the nervous system. It is also good for bronchitis and pain relief when it comes to coughs, GI issues, and menstrual cramps.

**ANNATTO SEED** (Bixa Orellana)

**AKA** Achiote or Achiotillo or Bija or Urucum or Atsuete

Annatto has a nutty, floral aroma. The flavor is best described as mildly sweet and spicy, with some earthy, musky notes. Annatto is used to color soups, stews, and rice. Perfect for making flavored oils and pastes as a little goes a long way. If you like sweet flavors, it can be added to homemade cocoa or chocolate drinks.

**Magical Uses**

Add Annatto to your meal if you are looking to repel negative energy and enemies.

Annatto seeds can also be used to hide your intent from your enemies.

**Healing Qualities**

Annatto had been used to treat diabetes, diarrhea, fevers, and fluid retention.

**ARROWROOT** (Maranta Arundinacea)

**AKA** Arrowroot Flour

Arrowroot is neutral tasting and is a great replacement for wheat flour. Mix in some almond or coconut flour or just use as is; for baking breads or cakes. Arrowroot is also a good thickening agent for puddings, sauces, soups, and gravy but be careful when adding to dairy as too much can ruin your texture.

**Magical Uses**

Add Arrowroot to your meal if you are seeking good fortune. While consuming the dish, picture a spinning arrow. As you finish the meal, imagine the arrow slowing down, and eventually coming to a stop, pointing straight ahead. Pay attention in the following days to dream as well as real-world signs showing you the way to find your fortune.

**Healing Qualities**

Arrowroot is gluten-free, and is good for the heart, blood circulation, and high cholesterol. Arrowroot cookies will do wonders for teething babies with itchy gums.

**ASAFOETIDA** (Ferula Assafoetida)

**AKA** Hing spice or Asafetida or Devil's Dung or Stinking Gum

Asafoetida is a prized spice in India and Iran where it is used (with discretion) to flavor curries, meatballs, and pickles. It adds a strong onion-like odor to any dish.

**Magical Uses**

Asafoetida is used to gain insight. After consumption, you will find that you have better understanding of people and situations. Effects can last between several days and several weeks depending on whether you have natural empathetic abilities and what level they are.

Or consume a dish of asafetida to banish negative energy and unwelcome spirits.

**Healing Qualities**

Asafoetida can be used as an antidote to opium. Note that this does not replace medical help in the case of overdosing.

## ASHWAGANDHA (Withania Somnifera)

**AKA** India Winter Cherry or Indian Ginseng

Because of its bitter taste, you want to use this in cookie recipes, and recipes that contain a lot of cocoa. Ashwagandha can also be added to sweet fruit smoothies.

### Magical Uses

Ashwagandha aids in revitalization of the spirit and reestablishing emotional balance. Use this root if you are struggling to find balance between your heart, mind, and soul.

### Healing Qualities

Ashwagandha is used for stress relief, hormone balance, mental health, and can promote restful sleep.

**NOTE**: Please do not feed this to anyone pregnant or breastfeeding, nor should it be consumed by individuals with autoimmune diseases.

## ASTRAGALUS ROOT (Astragalus Membranaceus)

**AKA** Huang Qi or Milkvetch

Astragalus Root has a garlic-like odor and an earthy taste. Making it a nice edition to soups, stews, and broths, but do not use a heavy hand. A little really goes a long way with this root.

### Magical Uses

Add Astragalus Root to your meal if you are looking for mental and physical rejuvenation. It can provide a real boost after exams, big moves, divorce, or just a very taxing week.

### Healing Qualities

Adding Astragalus Root to your diet can increase longevity, energy, and general physical health.

B

**BAY LEAF** (LAURUS NOBILIS)

**AKA** Bay Laurel or Sweet Bay

Add this herb to soups, stews, braised dishes, or as part of a meat rub. The flavor may start out harsh with hints of menthol, it does mellow as it continues to cook. The result is a subtle flavor that will remind you of black tea, oregano, and thyme. Bay leaves also contain a number of enzymes that help break down certain properties in beans and meat, making them easier to digest and reduces gas.

If you use the leaf as a whole, remember to remove before eating, but don't worry because all the magical goodness will have cooked into the food.

**Magical Uses**

Bay leaves are used to assist with manifestation and wish granting. Use mental manifestation techniques while eating, focusing your thoughts and feelings into what it is you really want.

Bay leaves can also help increase or attract inspiration. Unlike with the manifestation technique, allow your mind to wonder wherever it pleases as you eat your bay infused dish.

**Healing Qualities**

Bay leaves have anti-inflammatory properties, aid with digestion, migraines, and promote general health.

**BASIL** (Ocimum Basilcum)

AKA Albahaca or Basilic or Basilici Herba or Common Basil or Garden Basil or Krishna Tulsi or Munjariki or Ocimum Basilicum or St. Josephwort or Surasa or Sweet Basil or Vanatulasi or Varvara or Visva Tulsi

Basil hovers between sweet and savory with a very mild peppery undertone. You cannot make pesto without basil; and it adds a distinctive flavor to salads, pasta, and pizza.

**Magical Uses**

Cook with basil if you are interested in improving the quality of love and sympathy you experience.

Basil can attract wealth.

It is also good for adding a layer of protection or to dispel confusion and fears.

On special occasions, use basil to heighten sex drive and the bond formed during sex.

Consume in a dish twenty minutes before divination for accuracy and clarity.

**Healing Qualities**

Basil aids against high blood pressure and helps fight inflammation in the body and can help lower the risk of heart disease and arthritis.

**BEETROOT POWDER** (Beta Vulagris)

**AKA** Beet Powder

This vivid purple powder is mild, earthy, and moderately sweet. Beetroot powder will liven up any sauce, smoothie, or dough. It is easily masked by other spices and cocoa, making it a great ingredient for baking chocolate muffins and cakes or to liven up your hot cocoa topped with marshmallows.

**Magical Uses**

Beetroot powder is the very symbol of love and outer beauty, so add it to your meal if you wish to increase either of these in your life.

**Healing Qualities**

Beetroot powder can help with attention problems and in lessening hyperactivity. It can lower blood pressure, blood cholesterol, and blood sugar.

## BERGAMOT (Monarda Fistulosa)

**AKA** (Purple) Bee Balm or Wild Purple Bergamot

Not to be confused with Scarlet Bee Balm (Also referred to as Wild Bergamot), or their citrus fruit-bearing tree cousin. Bergamot has a similar smell to Greek oregano. And just like oregano, you can add dried bergamot to your tomato base or pizza sauce. You should also consider adding this herb to bread doughs and pastries. Or try mixing sliced fresh leaves (or flowers) into potato salad, soups, stews, beans, marinades, tomato sauce, eggs, seafood, or meat.

### Magical Uses

Cook with Bergamot if want to dispel depression, gloom, and sadness from your life.

### Healing Qualities

Bergamot helps fight colds, flu, upper respiratory problems, gas, diarrhea, nausea, fevers, and whooping cough.

## BERGAMOT, WILD (Monarda Didyma)

**AKA** (Scarlet) Bee Balm

This form of Bergamot flower has similar citrus notes to its fruit-bearing tree cousin. Perfect for tea breads and summer cakes.

### Magical Uses

Cook with Bergamot if want to invite prosperity, abundance, and happiness into your life.

### Healing Qualities

This form of Bergamot can help ease digestive and respiratory symptoms, as well as lower fever. It also a mild menstrual regulator.

## BLACK CUMIN (Nigella Sativa)

**AKA** Black Seed or Black Caraway or Roman Coriander or Kalonji or Fennel Flower or Love-in-mist.

Black Cumin has an earthy, almost nutty taste with a hint of citrus. Add black Cumin to your (savory) dough of choice, or sprinkle on fish with lemon to enhance the citrus smell and taste. It can be added to sauces, salads, and vegetables.

### Magical Uses

Use Black Cumin in your cooking for protection against spiritual attacks and from self-harming thoughts.

Black Cumin can increase the bond of love between you and whoever you are sharing the meal with.

### Healing Qualities

Black Cumin aids in digestion, provides iron, as well as stabilizing blood sugar, and blood pressure levels.

## BLACK MUSTARD (Brassicaceae Nigra)

**AKA** True Mustard

Black Mustard seeds have a pungent and spicy aroma, but fry them in some oil and you release a nutty aroma and give them a sweet and mild taste. They complement any curry or stir fry.

### Magical Uses

Black Mustard is a must for banishing and protection. It will help scrub you from the thoughts and tongues of those who wish you ill and shield you against the Evil Eye.

### Healing Qualities

Black mustard is known to hasten along common colds, relieve joint, and muscle pain such as rheumatism and arthritis.

## BLACK PEPPER (Piper Nigrum)

**AKA** N/A

Black pepper has a woody aroma and a bit of a bite. Black pepper is a super versatile ingredient and can add flavor and spice to meats, fish, vegetables, salad dressings, soups, stir-fries, pasta, and basically any savory dish you can think of.

**Magical Uses**

Black pepper can be added to food to dispel jealousy and to promote courage, as well as warding off negative energy and banishing mild curses.

**Healing Qualities**

Black pepper boosts brain function. It may help improve blood sugar control and lower cholesterol levels.

**BLACKBERRY LEAF** (Rubus fruticosus)

**AKA** N/A

Mild, fruity, and sometimes bitter; if you are using blackberry leaves in your tea, you might want to add honey. Another option is to add thin strips to your fruit salad.

**Magical Uses**

Blackberry leaves can help those battling evil spirits or personal inner demons. Consume during sunset for the best results.

**Healing Qualities**

Chew fresh blackberry leaves to aid in improving gum health, sore throats and mouth ulcers. These leaves also have a long history in aiding against sinusitis and anemia. Blackberry leaf can also provide relief of symptoms that come with menstruation, diarrhea, dysentery, cystitis, and hemorrhoids.

**BORAGE** (Borago Officinalis)

**AKA** Star Flower or Bee Bush

The taste of borage lingers somewhere between cucumber and oyster mushrooms and brings a unique flavor to salads, soups, and sauces.

**Magical Uses**

Add Borage to food if you wish to increase courage and innate psychic abilities. Works especially well when the abilities in question are inherited.

**Healing Qualities**

Borage is used to promote healthy skin, and combat depression with sedative-like qualities similar to those found in tryptophan (turkey), but not as severe.

**BROWN MUSTARD** (Brassica Juncea)

**AKA** Indian Mustard or Chinese Mustard or Oriental Mustard or Leaf Mustard or Vegetable Mustard.

Medium heat, brown mustard has a malty taste and can be added to salad dressings, vinaigrettes, basting, barbecue sauce, gravy, potato salad, and coleslaw.

**Magical Uses**

Add brown mustard to bring positivity, and boost the ability of attracting and manifesting good things into your life through positive thoughts. Remember to feel gratitude while eating.

**Healing Qualities**

Brown mustard can aid in lowering blood sugar and help against infections.

**BURNET** (Sanguisorba Minor)

**AKA** Salad Burnet or Garden Burnet or Small Burnet or Pimpernel or Toper's plant or Burnet-bloodwort.

With a nutty, cucumber taste, burnet is best used in salads or as a garnish for gin and tonic.

**Magical Uses**

Add burnet to your meal to strengthen platonic love and friendship.

**Healing Qualities**

Burnet can aid in lowering blood sugar and help against inflammation.

C

**CANNABIS** (Cannabaceae)

**AKA** Marijuana or Weed

This topic on its own can take up several books, but we are just going to keep it simple. The two main species consumed by humans are Cannabis Indica and Cannabis Sativa. While each has a list of distinctive health benefits, it is good to remember that Indica can induce what we call a body high and has a relaxing effect, where Sativa is more a head high that stimulates your mind and provides mental, as well as physical, energy. So, if you are cooking for a party, Indica is not the best option, or it should be reserved for dessert when you want your guests to start winding down before you send them home.

To activate all the goodness found inside this herb, it must first go through a heating process called decarboxylation (decarb or decarbing for short) which is done in the oven. If you are working with wild dry herbs, be sure to soak the ground up matter in water and exchange the water for clean water every six to twelve hours until the water runs clear. This process can take a few days but is needed if you wish to remove excess dirt and chlorophyll, and have better tasting herbs to work with.

Cannabis tastes varies from strain to strain, from earthy to citrus and everything in between. If you are picking a herb out to add to a meal, and have a variety to choose from, do the sniff test and go with your nose. Cannabis is covered in terpenes

(terpenes are responsible for smells and flavors) and filled with cannabinoids. Depending on what cannabinoids your body is lacking, the receptors in your nose will find those terpenes particularly appealing.

The cooking and baking possibilities are endless, but cannabis is most effective when used with fats, butters, and oils.

**Magical Uses**

Add cannabis to your dishes when you are trying to invoke energy healing, chakra activation, and increase psychic awareness. Even meditation can be improved by consuming a cannabis infused dish about 45 minutes beforehand.

Eat before entering a meditative state for a tulpa creation session. It will stimulate creativity and assist with the visualization process, creating for stronger, more fully formed tulpas.

**Healing Qualities**

This versatile plant can help lessen anxiety, stress, and sleep problems. It can also reduce the risk of chronic illnesses such as cancer, mood disorders, neurological disorders, digestive problems, nausea, muscle spasms, epilepsy, and skin conditions.

**NOTE**: If you are inexperienced, be careful how much you eat. Rather consume small amounts or single portions, and wait 45 minutes before deciding on a second portion.

**CARROWAY SEEDS** (Carum Carvi)

**AKA** Meridian Fennel and Persian Cumin

Carroway seeds have an almost nutty taste that can easily be confused with anise, but with a hint of citrus. It goes particularly well with chives, cumin, dill, thyme, and parsley. The carroway seed works best when added to stews and other meaty dishes, but is fun to experiment with when baking health breads, biscuits, and cakes.

## Magical Uses

Add Carroway seeds to your meal if you are looking to boost innate or awaken latent magical abilities.

It is also helpful in remembering and retrieving memories, or enhancing the clarity of old faded ones. Fair warning to be weary of retrieving suppressed memories, especially ones you suspect might be violent. Rather, talk to someone skilled in the art of hypnosis for assistance. It can also be helpful when attempting past life regression.

If you are sharing a meal for two with someone you care for, the carroway seed can help protect against fidelity as well as increase the level of passion, and reinforce feelings attached to old and new shared memories.

## Healing Qualities

Carroway Seeds are gentle on the digestive tract, assisting with problems such as heartburn, bloating, gas, loss of appetite, and mild stomach or intestinal cramping.

## CARDAMON (Elettaria Cardamomum)

**AKA** Cardamom or Green Cardamom or Capalaga or Ilachi or True Cardamom or Ceylon Cardamom

Cardamom's fruity and almost woody aroma makes it a perfect companion to citrus flavors. Its warmth and mild sweetness can put an interesting spin on classic savory poultry and red meat dishes. It's a must have for curries. When it comes to winter, add nutmeg and cinnamon to create a mixed spice blend, before adding to recipes for warm puddings, tea breads and pumpkin dishes.

## Magical Uses

You will want to add a little cardamom if you are planning a romantic evening. Not only does it increase sexual desire, and strengthen existing bonds of love, but it can help protect against thoughts of the unfaithful nature.

If you are worried about your lover's wondering eye, or if you worry others might tempt him away, gift your loved one with a magical gift infused with cardamom. Cookies, biscuits, and rusks work well. Tell your lover to think of you every time he or she eats one. Do this once a month.

**Healing Qualities**

Cardamom has vitamin C, magnesium, potassium, and it's high in antioxidants, giving you more reason to use around winter to help against the common cold, the flu, and sore throats.

**CATNIP** (Nepeta Cataria)

**AKA** Catmint or Catwort or Field Balm

Catnip has an almost sweet and minty scent, and tastes woodsy with a hint of citrus. To get the best out of your fresh catnip, try soaking it in lemon. The longer you soak it, the more of a minty citrus taste it will have. We use the leaves and shoots of fresh catnip in salads, soups, sauces and beef, lamb, or turkey dishes.

**Magical Uses**

Catnip is used for protection while sleeping, helping against nightmares, night terrors, and sleep paralysis

Catnip can also aid those struggling to remember dreams, learning to astral travel, lucid, and mutual dreaming, or new to graveyard walking and death stalking. Consume at least twenty minutes before attempting or practicing any of the aforementioned to help notice, interpret, and understand any attempts of communication or messages that come your way.

**Healing Qualities**

Catnip aids in digestion and catnip tea is regularly used to help babies suffering with colic.

**CAYENNE PEPPER** (Capsicum Annuum)

**AKA** Chile Pepper or Red chili

Despite its mild aroma, cayenne pepper is hot and fiery with an earthy taste. Always add to taste, so as not to overdo it, but this spice is so versatile you can use it with meat, fish, chicken, vegetarian, and chocolate dishes.

**Magical Uses**

Need a little spice in the bedroom? Cayenne Pepper will definitely turn up the heat.

Or if you are worried your dinner party being a little bland, then a dish with Cayenne pepper is a sure-fire path to an evening of easy and lighthearted fun.

Cayenne pepper can help someone struggling with shyness, but it needs to be eaten five to seven times a week until desired effect has taken place.

**Healing Qualities**

Cayenne Pepper can help lower blood pressure while promoting weight loss. Also high in vitamin C and antioxidants, this is a winter must-have.

**CELERY SEEDS** (Apium graveolens)

**AKA** Ajmod

Warm and bitter in taste with an earthy aroma, sprinkle over salad, and stir into hearty casseroles or add to your spice rub when you plan on grilling meat.

**Magical Uses**

Celery seeds are good if you need a boost in mental and psychic powers, or need increased concentration during a ritual. In the case of the latter, if you are not performing the ritual alone, invite those joining you to assist with making and partaking in the dinner to strengthen the outcome of the ritual.

**Healing Qualities**

Celery seeds can help improve blood pressure and water retention. It can ease arthritis and does behave as a very mild tranquilizer, assisting in short term stress.

## CEYLON CINNAMON (Cinnamomum Verum)

**AKA** Soft Cinnamon or True Cinnamon or Cinnamon

There is a very good chance you have this version of cinnamon in your kitchen. Softer in color than its cassia cousin, this spice is mild and delicate with an almost floral woody aroma and taste. You cannot make cinnamon rolls without Ceylon, nor can you eat a South African styled pancake without it. Easily add depth to curries, pumpkin pies, and hot chocolate with this light and delightful spice.

### Magical Uses

Turn your hot chocolate into an aphrodisiac with Ceylon cinnamon and turn it up a notch by adding a dash of red chili.

On the other hand, this spice is a must have around the holidays when used to create dishes that warms hearts and cools tempers.

Cinnamon is also wonderful if you are looking for a little magnetism. It will make people feel drawn to you, more trusting of you, and more comfortable around you. Do not be surprised if people start opening up to you more often.

### Healing Qualities

Ceylon may help in the fight against heart disease and is a wonderful antioxidant. Unlike its cassia cousin, Ceylon cinnamon does not have the potential to cause liver failure, meaning you can safely consume Ceylon on a regular basis. It is also good for lowering blood pressure.

## CHIA SEEDS (Salvia Hispanica)

**AKA** Mexican Chia or Salba Chia

Chia seeds will take on the flavor of whatever ingredients you lump it in with, and they will swell to several times their normal size when liquids are introduced. Be sure to add them to salads, smoothies, and baked goods like bread and muffins.

**Magical Uses**

Whether you are going through a tough time, or generally very sensitive emotionally, or a fully-fledged empath that is in need of a little mental protection, or a way to increase mental endurance, then chia seeds are for you.

**Healing Qualities**

If you are looking out for your gut health, then add chia seeds to your diet. It also aids in weight loss because of its high fiber content, it leaves you feeling satisfied for longer. It is also recommended for those suffering high blood pressure.

**CHERVIL** (Anthriscus Cerefolium)

**AKA** French Parsley

Mild like parsley, but with the warmth reminiscent of anise, this tender herb is best used with fish, poultry, or soup.

**Magical Uses**

Are you preparing for a battle of wits? Or perhaps an exam or an interview? Then add a little chervil to sharpen the mind.

Chervil can also help you keep focus on a particular goal in mind; this is very helpful to those who get demotivated easily or who suffer bouts of laziness.

**Healing Qualities**

Can be taken as a mild stimulant or mood enhancer. Not bad for gout flair-ups either.

**CHICORY** (Cichorium intybus)

AKA Blue Daisy or Blue Sailor or Wild Bachelor's Button, Blue Dandelion or Italian Dandelion or Coffeeweed

The roots are bitter until roasted, giving them a wild-coffee smell, along with a woody and nutty taste. Add sautéed chicory to chicken, pork, or roasts, or add it along with pear or green apple to any green salad.

**Magical Uses**

Use chicory if you need to stay invisible to your enemy or destroy mental blocks.

Chicory can help with perseverance.

**Healing Qualities**

Chicory can stimulate kidneys and urine output, and can counter the effect of mild caffeine overdose.

**CHILI PEPPER** (Capsicum Frutescens)

**AKA** Hot Peppers or Chili

They come in all shapes, sizes, colors, and spiciness that can range from mild to warm to volcanic. They can also be used in a variety of meat, poultry, vegetable, and curry dishes, as well as sauces, dips, and gravy. Any dish you fear is too plain, can be transformed into something completely new with just a dash of chili.

**Magical Uses**

If you are in need of magical protection against evil spirits and negative energies, add chili pepper.

Chili is a must for adding spice to your sex life.

**Healing Qualities**

Packed with vitamins and minerals, a little chili is also known for speeding up the healing time of stomach ulcers.

**CHIVES** (Allium Schoenoprasum)

**AKA** Onion Chives or Wild Chives or Cives

A hardy herb, chives have a mild onion and herb, smell and taste, even more so than green onions. It is a very popular ingredient for dips. You can add chives to salad, but it goes particularly well with potato dishes, soups, fish, and other seafood dishes. To get the best out of your chives flavor-wise, thinly slice and leave to air for a moment or two; and remember that heat kills its flavor, so when it comes to warm dishes, always add it last minute.

**Magical Uses**

Planning on doing a reading? Whether tea leaves, palmistry, or cards, add chives to your meal beforehand to bring your divination to a new level. It will also help with repelling any evil spirits attracted to you during the reading.

Chives are also good for general protection against bad luck and negative energy.

**Healing Qualities**

If you are at risk of Alzheimer's, adding chives to your diet could help aid your fight against it as this herb is renowned for improving memory functions.

**CILANTRO** (Coriandrum Sativum)

**AKA** Coriander or Chinese Parsley or Dhania

Cilantro is a tender herb with tart tasting leaves that have a citrus undertone, while the seeds are earthier and become sweet when roasted. When making sausage from scratch, you cannot forget your cilantro seeds. Whether you are planning on making beef, chick, fish, pork, or veal, this versatile herb will enhance the natural flavors.

**Magical Uses**

This is great for gardeners, especially those growing and consuming their own cilantro and other herbs or vegetables. It deepens the spiritual connection to the earth, flowers, vegetables, and herbs in your garden and nature in general.

Cilantro will also strengthen any earth magics like rain dances and animal guide summoning, or nature spirits and animal communication spells, performed within three hours of eating.

**Healing Qualities**

Rich in antioxidants, add cilantro to your diet to just generally keep up (and improve on) good health and skin. Also recommended for those with high blood pressure.

**CINNAMON CASSIA** (Cinnamomum Cassia)

**AKA** Chinese Cinnamon or False Cinnamon

Not to be confused with Ceylon cinnamon, Cassia is dark in color and has a spicy and earthy aroma and taste. This spice is best used in savory dishes but also works with dark chocolate and liqueurs.

**Magical Uses**

You can easily attract success, power, prosperity, and luck with this common household spice, but be warned not to consume it too often as it might cause the opposite effect.

**Healing Qualities**

Cassia is great for joint pain and menstrual cramps, but just as with its magical use, it comes with a warning, or in this case two: This spice is NOT to be consumed by pregnant women, nor should anyone consume it on a daily basis as high amounts can cause liver damage.

**CLOVES** (Syzygium Aromaticum)

**AKA** Zobo Pepper

Spicy and sweet, warm and woodsy; it's no wonder cloves bring warmth to any dish they are added to. Poke them into ham or chicken, but you might want to use this spice in mulled wine, stewed fruit, pumpkin pie, and gingerbread.

**Magical Uses**

To enhance spells, add cloves to the meal you eat prior to casting. It can also be used to drive away loneliness.

**Healing Qualities**

Cloves can help reduce the risk of developing diabetes, heart disease, and certain cancers. It detoxifies while giving you an immune boost.

**COSTMARY** (Tanacetum Balsamita)

**AKA** Bible Leaf or Ale cost

Either a mild bitter lemon or mildly minty in taste, costmary is used fresh in salads, or as a dried herb for fish, chicken, and other poultry.

**Magical Uses**

Consume costmary if you need to clear or awaken your psychic sense. It can also be consumed for reinvigorating auras or before attempting a chakra realignment.

**Healing Qualities**

Costmary can assist with coughs, colds, and stomach cramps.

**NOTE:** Not to be consumed by pregnant women. Can be used to ease and treat the discomforts of dysentery.

**CUMIN** (Cuminum Cyminum)

**AKA** Cummin

With a warm, nutty aroma and slightly peppery in taste, cumin gives an earthiness to Indian curry, chili con carne, soups, stews, and breads.

**Magical Uses**

Use Cumin to attract a lover and rouse sexual desires. It can also help protect a summoner from possession if consumed beforehand.

**Healing Qualities**

Cumin can help if you are suffering from an immune system disorder or allergies.

**CURRY LEAVES** (Murraya Koenigii)

**AKA** Sweet Neem

Do not let the name fool you, as the leaf doesn't smell like curry at all! The curry leaf is warm with a complex grassy citrus flavor and a taste that reminds you of the sub-tropical climate the curry tree grows in. This curry leaf is an obvious must have if you want your curry to create a flavor explosion with every mouthful.

**Magical Uses**

Adding curry leaves to your meal will help dispel any evil forces you may have brought home from the graveyard, or inadvertently summoned, released, or attracted during a reading.

**Healing Qualities**

Curry leaves are a very helpful addition to your diet if you are suffering stomach problems, nausea, or morning sickness.

D

**DILL** (Anethum Graveolens)

**AKA** Dill Weed

Dill is a tender herb that is citrusy with a feel of summer, this works well with salmon, potatoes, and mushroom dishes, but you can add it to pretty much any green vegetable dish.

**Magical Uses**

Dill can help bring balance between our heart and head.

It should also be consumed if you think someone is sending negative energies, casting the Evil Eye or curses your way. If you feel you are sending out negative energies into the world, dill can help put a stop to that and assist in neutralizing self-generated negative energy.

**Healing Qualities**

Good for cholesterol and heart disease, adding dill to your diet may also help against strokes.

F

**FENNEL** (Foeniculum Vulgare)

**AKA** Sweet Anise or Finnochio or Florentine Fennel or Florence Fenne

Licorice flavor, fennel pairs best with pork and seafood.

**Magical Uses**

Consume for courage and to help repair a broken heart.

Aids in sensing nature spirits.

**Healing Qualities**

Good for heartburn and gas.

**FENUGREEK** (Trigonel la foenum-graecum)

**AKA** Foenugreek or Metchi or Alholva, Bird's Foot or Bockshornklee or Bockshornsame or Chandrika or Fenogreco or Greek Clover or Greek Hay or Hu Lu Ba or Medhika or Sénégrain or Trigonella or Woo Lu Bar

Tangy and bitter, fenugreek is mostly used in curries, stews, lentils, and potato dishes.

**Magical Uses**

Fenugreek is used by seers to hone their skills and for grounding.

**Healing Qualities**

Fenugreek can lower cholesterol and blood sugar levels, as well as increase milk production in lactating mothers.

**Filé** (Sassafras albidum)

**AKA** Gumbo Filé

Spicy and similar to thyme, this spice is an essential for Gumbo or potjie pot, but be sure to add it right at the end to not ruin its texture.

**Magical Uses**

This spice is said to attract warmth into your life.

**Healing Qualities**

A great anti-inflammatory, filé can also help relieve arthritis and gout.

G

**GARLIC** (Allium Sativum)

**AKA** N/A

Pungent, with a biting taste when eaten raw, and while it might not be great for romance, it brings a sweetness to any savory dish. Crush or chop finely for stronger flavor, cook for longer if you prefer something that a little more mellow.

**Magical Uses**

Garlic repels negativity and is great for cleansing. A little goes far, and a single clove in a dish that serves two is more than enough. It also guards against theft and illness.

Usually eaten in a meal before going on a graveyard walk so to shield against possession or attaching spirits.

**Healing Qualities**

Garlic is known for helping halt formation and growth of cancer cells. It also boosts the immune system, reduces high blood pressure, reduces cholesterol and may prevent Alzheimer's and Dementia. It is also good for sinus sufferers, and improving gut health by keeping 'bad' bacteria levels low and under control.

It might be good to know that garlic is mildly poisonous to humans. The more you reek of garlic after consumption, the more allergic you are.

\*\*\*

**GINGER** (Zingiber Officinale)

**AKA** N/A

Spicy, warm and invigorating, use ginger in stir fry or baked goods like ginger-snaps or ginger bread men. If you are making fruit beer, add some ginger during the fermentation process for that extra zing.

**Magical Uses**

Consume for spiritual healing or protection from evil, and you should consume ginger before doing a cleansing or death stalking as it will help you consume less energy during the event. Ginger can also warm, lighten, and soften a heart. This is particularly helpful over a holiday period.

**Healing Qualities**

Ginger helps against germs, congestion, and chronic sinus; soothes nausea, eases period pains, and stimulates the digestive system. You should add ginger to your diet if you are fighting cancer or have high blood pressure problems.

**GRAINS OF PARADISE** (Aframomum Melegueta)

**AKA** Guinea Grains or Melegueta or Guinea Pepper or Alligator Pepper

Warm and spicy with an aroma that is almost floral, it pairs well with your woodsy spices like cinnamon and ginger. This spice brings warmth to winter soups and dishes.

**Magical Uses**

Consume to increase luck and success. For those with natural abilities, it will temporarily heighten empathy and divination accuracy, while preventing the emotional drain that usually comes with it.

**Healing Qualities**

Grains of Paradise not only helps with inflammation, but with weight loss too.

H

**HEMP** (Cannabis Sativa ssp. Sativa)
**AKA** N/A

While hemp does smell and taste a lot like cannabis, the two need to be heated a little differently. That said, raw hemp leaves can be added to salads, most savory dishes, or fruit tea.

Dry it out at the recommended temperature, crush and bottle, and there you have an aromatic herb that pairs well with any dry green herbs like thyme or basil. It's especially good when making pasta or pizza.

On the other side, it works brilliantly in baked goods, especially of the vanilla, chocolate, or peanut butter variety. Though for the best taste and texture, infuse butter with hemp and strain out the herb before using.

Keep the seeds aside and crush before adding them to stews, meat rubs, and pastas; or add to your flour, herb, and spice mixture for fried chicken.

**Magical Uses**

Hemp detaches negative energies from your body.

It can help you maintain a balance of power over evil when consumed regularly.

Hemp can assist with negative psychic attacks.

If you feel consumed by negativity, to the point where it is no longer just attached to you but where you can almost feel it in your bones do the following: bake a batch of biscuits with hemp infused butter. Eat one every 30 minutes before taking a hot shower or bath (preferably before bed). While you wash, imagine you are washing the negativity from you. Afterwards, find a quiet and comfortable space and have a short meditation session, or go straight to bed and expect a good night's sleep.

**Healing Qualities**

Where cannabis is known for its psychoactive qualities, hemp has more of an effect on the body. Especially when consumed under the right conditions, hemp provides a 'body' high. Eat it raw and benefit from its high nutritional value.

It is also perfect for aches and pains, no matter where they originate from. It reduces the risk of heart diseases, reduces cholesterol, regulates blood pressure, promotes healthy and glowing skin, aids digestion, and promotes restful sleep.

To get the best health benefits, especially in the way of pain relief, bake at 240 degrees Fahrenheit or 115 degrees Celsius for 90 minutes before adding or using as an ingredient.

**HOLY BASIL** (Ocimum Tenuiflorum)

**AKA** Tulsi or Tulasi or Hot Basil

Unlike regular basil with its sweet taste, holy basil is peppery with a hint of mint. Combine this herb with garlic and chilies and use it to flavor fish, chicken, meat, or potato dishes.

**Magical Uses**

For energy balance and chakra realignment, add holy basil to your meal.

**Healing Qualities**

Holy basil can protect you against infection, lower cholesterol, and blood sugar. It is also a helpful herb to those suffering stomach ulcers as it lowers the acid level.

**HOREHOUND** (Marrubium Vulgare)

AKA Hoarhound or White Horehound

With a taste similar to root beer with a licorice twist, these leaves and flowers are best used to flavor hard candies, alcoholic beverages, and sodas.

**Magical Uses**

Horehound can provide mental clarity and is consumed for this reason before rituals. It can also be used for those seeking a little inspiration or boost in their creativity.

If you find yourself facing exhaustion from constant decisions all day, then keep a stash of horehound hard candies. When you need a mental pick-me-up or help making choices, treat yourself to one.

**Healing Qualities**

Horehound does wonders for digestion problems such as gas and indigestion. Turn it into a candy or tea to soothe coughs and break down mucus build-up caused by sinus. Be sure not to consume too much as it can induce vomiting in some people.

**HYSSOP** (Hyssopus Officinalis)

**AKA** Herbe de Joseph or Herbe Sacrée or Herbe Sainte or Hiope or Hisopo or Jufa or Rabo De Gato or Ysop

Sweet smelling and with a warm mint taste, you can use Hyssop to flavor soups and in stuffing, or shred finely and add sugar to create a range of jams, candies, and fruit-infused syrups.

**Magical Uses**

For a heart broken by death, and for those struggling with haunted and heavy thoughts about those lost, hyssop can smooth and hasten along the healing process. Turn into a syrup or jam and serve at wakes and funerals.

**Healing Qualities**

Hyssop can ease colic, coughs, colds, and other respiratory problems.

## L
**LAVENDER** (Lavandula)

**AKA** True Lavender or English Lavender

Pretty to look at in both fresh and dry forms, this woodsy floral herb can add color and flavor to lamb, fruit salads, desserts, cakes, teas, and ice cream.

### Magical Uses

By consuming lavender, you are attracting peace into your life. Consume before attempting meditation or astral traveling, if you struggle to relax your mind.

### Healing Qualities

Lavender can help improve sleep, reduce blood pressure, and ease menopausal flushes.

**LEMON BALM** (Melissa Officinalis)

**AKA** Bee balm or Cure-all or Dropsy Plant or Honey Plant or Melissa or Melissa Folium or Sweet Mary

Combine lemon and soft mint, and you get a good idea of what lemon balm smells and tastes like. It gives stuffing and salads a summer kick, and you cannot go wrong adding it to fish, poultry, or crisp vegetable dishes.

### Magical Uses

Use lemon balm to bring out the happiness in each of your guests. It's also fantastic if you need to calm a busy mind and spirit.

### Healing Qualities

Lemon balm can help you beat low levels of stress and anxiety, and combat insomnia.

**LEMON GRASS** (Cymbopogon Citratus)

**AKA** Oil Grass or Fresh Lemongrass

Like the name suggests, Lemon Grass has a citrus taste, but with a ginger kick. It can be used as a substitute for lemon and is often used in salads but don't shy away from using it with roasted meats and curry.

**Magical Uses**

If you are preparing a romantic dinner with the intention of heading to the bedroom after, add some lemongrass for sexual satisfaction.

**Healing Qualities**

Lemongrass can relieve pain and help with fever. It also aids against high blood pressure.

**LEMON VERBENA** (Aloysia Citriodora)

**AKA** Lemon Beebrush

Mildly sweet and lemony, lemon verbena pairs well with savory roasts and poultry, and equally well with ice-creams, summer desserts, and jams.

**Magical Uses**

Consume for beauty, or before charm creation and spell casting for a stronger outcome.

**Healing Qualities**

This herb can help with sleep problems and low levels of stress.

**LICORICE** (Glycyrrhiza Glabra)

**AKA** Liquorice or Sweet Root

Similar, yet sweeter than anise, licorice can be used in anything from soups to stews, but is most popularly used to makes sweets and flavor both alcoholic and non-alcoholic beverages.

**Magical Uses**

Used to heighten the quality and strength of spell work when consumed beforehand. It will also strengthen the magical qualities of the other ingredients used in making the meal.

**Healing Qualities**

Licorice works well against bacterial and viral infections. Candy made from it can be given to teething babies but do keep in mind not to give infants small pieces of candy. Replace the potential choking hazard for strings of soft licorice (black licorice works best).

On the mental health side, licorice is a well-known for aiding in stress and anxiety relief.

**LOVAGE** (Levisticum Officinale)

**AKA** Smellage or Maggie Plant or Mountain Celery

It smells and tastes a bit like celery and parsley, except it is spicy. A fantastic addition to potatoes, pork, and poultry. Lovage can also add a zing to your soups and stuffing.

**Magical Uses**

This is another must have ingredient if you are planning an evening of lust, desire, and encouraged attraction.

**Healing Qualities**

Use lovage to treat jaundice and regulate menstruation.

M

**MACE** (Myristica Fragrans)

**AKA** Mace Blades or Aril

Sweet, woody, warm and more delicate than nutmeg, add mace to your pumpkin pies, sweet potato, or yam dishes. It also gives depth and warmth to baked goods like rusks, cakes, and donuts.

**Magical Uses**

Increase psychic powers and awareness when you add mace to your cooking,

### Healing Qualities

Mace can cure nausea and regulate your digestive system.

### MARJORAM (Origanum Majorana)

**AKA** Sweet Marjoram

Bittersweet flavor, marjoram is mainly used in hearty dishes and with roasts, oxtail, pork, fish, and potatoes.

### Magical Uses

Attract or improve on platonic love and friendships. A shared meal with marjoram can help solidify new friendships and covens.

### Healing Qualities

Marjoram can help treat respiratory illness and diarrhea.

### MUGWORT (Artemisia Vulgaris)

**AKA** Elon herb or Chrysanthemum Weed or Wild Wormwood or Old Uncle Henry or Muggons or Old Man or Moxa or Cronewort or Sailor's Tobacco or St John's plant

Bitter tasting, mugwort smells a bit like sage. It's best used with fatty fish, meat, and poultry dishes.

### Magical Uses

Add mugwort to amplify psychic vision and induce prophetic dreaming.

### Healing Qualities

Use mugwort for digestive problems and to resolve irregular menstruation.

N

### NUTMEG (Myristica Fragrans)

**AKA** Musky Nut

Warm and slightly sweet, this spice goes well with winter dishes and baked goods. Nutmeg can be added to everything from meats to sausages, potatoes, vegetables (especially those from the pumpkin family), to baked goods, and winter puddings.

**Magical Uses**

Use it to clear any fog from your second sight, or to attract abundance and love into your life.

Empaths who feel depleted after dealing with people all day can enjoy a spiritual and mental replenishment when consuming nutmeg. An easy way to do this is with nutmeg tea, or biscuits flavored with the spice. Find a spot where you can enjoy your nutmeg treat in peace and quiet, and with every mouthful, concentrate on the taste and warmth of the nutmeg, and soon enough you will feel the emotional warmth spreading through you.

**Healing Qualities**

Nutmeg is known for its mood boosting properties but can be very beneficial to heart health and stabilizing sugar levels.

O

**OREGANO** (Origanum Vulgare)

**AKA** Organum or Wild Marjoram

Earthy, musty, and kind of sweet, oregano is a favorite in most kitchens. Use it fresh or dried by adding it to poultry, salad dressings, pasta, pizza, marinades, soups, vegetables, and legumes. Enhance its flavor by pairing it with tomatoes, feta cheese, and herbs like basil, mint, rosemary, and thyme.

**Magical Uses**

Promote good fortune and goodwill when you add oregano. The more goodwill you pass along, the more will come your way.

Add hope when there is none by adding oregano. Take time to breathe the flavors in before eating, as you do so, feel the good vibrations expand in your chest, and subsequently increase with every bite.

**Healing Qualities**

Lower cholesterol, pain, and improve on gut health with this versatile herb. It is also known to be able to slow down cancer growth.

P

**PAPRIKA** (Capsicum Annuum)

AKA N/A

There are three types of paprika: smoked, Spanish, and Hungarian. They range from mild to spicy, and sweet to savory. Paprika adds a fruity warmth to a meal of chicken, pork, or beef. You can also try adding it to mac and cheese, or cheese and tomato toasted sandwiches, for color and flair.

**Magical Uses**

Turn up the heat in the bedroom with paprika, or use to ensure your dinner party is not dull but smooth sailing with lighthearted fun.

**Healing Qualities**

Paprika can improve cholesterol and blood sugar levels. It is also linked to improving eye health.

**PARSLEY** (Petroselinum Crispum)

**AKA** Garden Parsley

This tender herb is fresh and grassy without being as robust as cilantro. Sauces, stews, burgers, sausages, pasta, and so many countless other dishes can benefit from a few sprigs of this herb.

**Magical Uses**

Ward off evil spirits with parsley. During times of war and strife, parsley can help ward off death and protect against the angry destructive energy of the world.

**Healing Qualities**

Parsley helps support bone growth and acts as a natural diuretic. Parsley prohibits cancer tumors from getting the nutrients they need to grow and survive.

**Mint** (Mentha × piperita)

**AKA** Peppermint

Mint is a tender herb, and a hybrid of water mint and spearmint. It has a sweet fragrance, a sweet minty taste and leaves in its wake a pleasant coolness. This works well with summer salads, pesto, and marinades, but if you want a real treat during those hot summer months, incorporate fresh mint into your homemade chocolate, ice-cream, or syrups.

**Magical Uses**

Consume in a meal before preforming animal magic, divination, cleansing, healing, or consecration, as mint will strengthen those types of magic. Also handy for stirring psychic energy, psychic development, enhancing connections (in the spiritual and waking world), and increases the chances of successful mutual dreaming and dream walking.

Add to the meal you plan to eat before traveling for a safe journey.

**Healing Qualities**

When eaten, peppermint can relieve stress and improve mental function. Also handy for coughs and sore throats when brewed as a tea.

**POPPY SEED** (Papaver Somniferum)

**AKA** Khus Khus

Poppy seeds have a nutty taste. Easiest incorporated into baked goods, either as a garnish on buns and breads, or as a main ingredient in rusks and lemon poppy seed muffins.

**Magical Uses**

The consumption of poppy seeds will help temporarily blind enemies and dark spirits from finding you.

To stay sharp of mind when facing an emissary or nemesis, consume thirty minutes before hand (be sure to check your teeth for any wayward seeds before speaking to anyone).

**Healing Qualities**

Increase cognitive function and bone health when you add poppies to your diet on a regular basis.

R

**ROSEMARY** (Salvia Rosmarinus)

**AKA** Compass Plant or Compass Weed or Encensier or Herbe Aux Couronnes or Old Man or Polar Plant or Romarin or Romarin Des Troubadours or Romero or Rose de Marie or Rose Des Marins or Rosée De Mer or Rosemarine or Rusmari or Rusmary

Rosemary is a hardy herb that tastes like a mix of lavender and sage with a mild lemony twist. Season chicken, game, or oily fish with fresh rosemary, or sprinkle the dried herb into mushroom and potato dishes.

**Magical Uses**

When memories turn sour from death or loss, a little rosemary will help turn the sadness into bitter sweetness.

Rosemary is also popular to gain the affections of someone. Share a meal with rosemary with the person if you want to stir feelings of love within them.

**Healing Qualities**

Boost your immune system and improve blood circulation by adding rosemary to your diet. Rosemary has properties that help prohibit the formation of tumors and breast cancer cells.

S

**SAFFRON** (Crocus Sativus)

**AKA** Zafran or Safran

Hovering between earthy and floral, saffron will compliment shellfish, risottos, stews, curries, almost any vegetable dish, and cream sauces.

**Magical Uses**

Add saffron to your cooking when you are trying to gain wealth, success, and affluence.

For the same reason, it is handy for those trying to find a rich husband. Consume it weekly to gain the attention of those with fortune, and when the time comes share a meal containing saffron with your potential lover to help seal the deal.

Be warned: Saffron does not take kindly to those who want only sex and fortune without any connection and love. If the partnership is deemed unfit, the spice will not allow for the relationship to continue, and bad endings can be expected.

**Healing Qualities**

Improve your mood and libido with saffron. Also known to improve high blood pressure problems.

**SAGE** (Salvia Officinalis)

**AKA** Culinary Sage or Common Garden Sage or Garden Sage.

This hardy herb is earthy and musky in aroma and taste. Use sage when cooking pork, poultry, or dishes involving root vegetables. If you are planning on baking or buying fresh bread, adding sage to homemade butter puts a refreshing spin on an old favorite.

## Magical Uses

Add sage to call wisdom and luck into your life, or simply if you need help with emotional healing, or lessoning the pains of grief.

## Healing Qualities

Sage can help with blood clotting and to improve brain function.

## SESAME (Sesamum Indicum)

**AKA** Benne

Sweet and nutty, you bring out the best of these seeds when they are baked or toasted. Crush and add to marinades, salads and dressings, stir fry, and vegetable dishes. You can also incorporate sesame seeds into health bread and bars, or sprinkle over buns before baking. Your other alternative is sesame oil, but be sure it is of high quality and remember that it is not interchangeable with the seeds themselves, when used in a recipe. The oil is still great when making salad dressing and marinades, and adds nice flavor to sautéed vegetables and meats.

## Magical Uses

Increase hope and lift spirits by incorporating sesame into food. It can also be used when seeking luck, and fortune. While the luck is real with no fallback, any fortunes are usually short lived so do not use for items that can break or be stolen, or for important investments.

## Healing Qualities

Sesame seeds can aid against arthritis pain, blood sugar control, and in lowering cholesterol. A spoonful of these seeds every other day work wonders on low estrogen levels.

## SORREL (Rumex Species)

**AKA** Common Sorrel or Garden Sorrel or Spinach Dock and Narrow-leaved Dock

Fruity and tart, this herb is best used in soups, spinach dishes, sprinkled in salads and in quiche.

**Magical Uses**

Sorrel can be used to attract joy but is mainly used to increase maternal affection in new mothers.

Serve a single dish with sorrel to a mother you suspect is suffering from 'baby blues'. It should lessen the feeling and help start or speed up the healing process. Do note that if you decide to magically get involved, you take responsibility to watch over the mother till she is well again. You can even ask other members of the coven to assist and take turns (as was once their duty, when women practitioners were synonymous with midwifes). If things escalate beyond your control, do not be afraid to advise professional help.

**Healing Qualities**

Sorrel is really high in antioxidants but don't consume in high doses, especially if you have a proclivity for kidney stones.

**STAR ANISE** (Illicium Verum)

**AKA** Star Aniseed and Chinese Star Anise

Star Anise is very sweet, peppery, and similar to anise. This herb is best used whole and in savory dishes, especially those that contain meat. You can also try adding it to soups, stews, and broths.

**Magical Uses**

Star anise should be consumed if you are seeking protection from the night and to lessen nightmares. It can also be used to increase passion, and love, as well as to improve or reveal latent psychic abilities.

**Healing Qualities**

Reduce symptoms of depression and menopause with star anise. It is also good for those who suffer regularly from stomach ulcers.

**SPEARMINT** (Mentha Spicata)

**AKA** Garden mint or Common Mint or Lamb Mint or Mackerel Mint

Fruity and minty, leaving a freshness in its wake, this soft herb can be used in summer soups, salads, cocktails, pesto, yogurt dips, and an array of warm or cold desserts and baked goods.

**Magical Uses**

Spearmint can be added when battling mild depression, and self-doubt. Add to meals if you suspect succubae or spirits have attached themselves to you, negatively impacting your life or if you are preparing to expel these entities.

**Healing Qualities**

Chew on some fresh spearmint leaves if you are suffering indigestion.

T

**TARRAGON** (Artemisia Dracunculus)

**AKA** Estragon or Dragon's Mugwort or Wyrmwort or Little Dragon

Vanilla mint with a peppery bite, add a sprinkle of this tender herb to vegetables about to be roasted, fish or chicken dishes.

**Magical Uses**

A very useful herb, tarragon can be used when you are in need of protection, or to heal your spiritual energy by replenishing your mana after an encounter with spirits. Consume in a meal before committing to a banishing.

Tarragon can also be used to draw luck and love into your life.

**Healing Qualities**

Tarragon helps with inflammation and to improve on sleep quality.

## THYME (Thymus Vulgaris)

**AKA** English Thyme or French Thyme or Garden Thyme

Woodsy, earthy, and surprisingly sweet, thyme can be used in almost every dish, meats, fish, chicken, vegetables, soups, marinades, savory baking, and so much more. Also, you can pair it with almost any herb or chili and most spices.

**Magical Uses**

Use thyme as often as you like to improve your connection with nature and to feel more grounded.

Eat before entering a meditative state for a tulpa creation session. The herb helps stabilize the process.

Thyme helps when experiencing problems connecting with the inner self, deciphering our wants and needs from the influences of others; or when we find it hard to hear our thoughts over the psychic and real chatter surround us. Add a teaspoon to your last meal of the day.

This herb can also provide protection against bad dreams and nightmares.

**Healing Qualities**

Drinking thyme tea can calm the nervous system, as well as doing a fine job at fighting a persistent cough. Some of the folk suffering with the early stages of dementia have found thyme to be helpful in the battle to slow the disease down.

## TUMERIC (Curcuma Longa)

**AKA** Haldi or Manjal or Curcumin

Usually bought in powder form, turmeric is dark yellow in color, has a mild earthy scent and a bitter taste, but don't let that put you off indulging in this aromatic spice to make delicious yellow rice or couscous.

**Magical Uses**

Consume turmeric for healing, strength and vitality.

**Healing Qualities**

**NOTE:** Consuming turmeric every day can interfere with your menstrual cycle.

It can help in the fight against excess free radicals that cause oxidative stress. Tumeric is also good for sinusitis, heart disease, and has anti-cancer properties.

## V

**VANILLA BEANS** (Vanilla Planifolia)

**AKA** N/A

This one needs little introduction. Vanilla beans will add a sweet taste and smell to custards, baked goods, milk drinks and ice-cream.

**Magical Uses**

Consume vanilla before hypnosis, astral travel or planned lucid dreaming, or if you are simply seeking sweeter dreams.

The other magical properties are more aimed at women, but great results are seen by anyone with truly feminine qualities.

Combine feminine magic and that found in vanilla, and you get a different sort of magic. Partake in premade vanilla snacks while performing beauty and glamour spells, or when you are having a non-magical pamper day with beauty treatments, or both! Vanilla will enhance the effect of the spells and treatments, allowing your inner beauty to shine through, and help you see yourself clearly all while guarding against vanity.

Feminine charm and magic do have their place. Someone imbued with these properties have a presence about them that attracts the eye and energy of those around them. Usually men, but not always. That masculine energy**Error! Bookmark not defined.** is directed back. Consuming vanilla with the intent of feminine charm on a regular basis ensures that some of that masculine energy (the positive and powerful parts) is absorbed and added to your natural and feminine energy

First, you need to understand the basic differences between feminine and masculine energy. Feminine energy is intuitive, creative, regenerating, restful, maternally protective, and driven by thought and heart. Masculine energy is assertive, strong, easily takes shape (materialization), and is driven by gut, logic, and fearlessness or bravery (depending on the situation). When you add a little bit of masculine energy to female energy, you find a balance that cancels out the more 'negative' side of feminine energy like over reflectiveness, over sacrificing, and action based on emotion. This brings for stronger magic, especially in spells of materialization, and low-grade natural shielding against negative energy and spiritual attacks.

**Healing Qualities**
Treat fever and spasms with vanilla.

W

**WASABI** (Eutrema Japonicum)

**AKA** Japanese Horseradish

Pungent and similar in taste to horseradish, wasabi can be used to spice up any dish or ground into a paste for sushi.

**Magical Uses**
Consume before banishing spells for strength and protection.

**Healing Qualities**
Wasabi is an anti-inflammatory that promotes weight loss.

**WHITE MUSTARD** (Sinapis Alba)

**AKA** Brassica Alba or B Hirta or Yellow Mustard

White mustard leaves have a peppery smell and taste, the powder form has no odor. Use white mustard in stir fry and with leafy green vegetable.

## Magical Uses

Consume if you need spiritual protection and before performing a banishment.

## Healing Qualities

White mustard can help relieve joint pain.

# Vegetables

To be fair, all vegetables are magic in the sense that they are good for you. They provide vitamins, minerals, and antioxidants, while helping to stave off or lower the risk of many diseases. While there are thousands of vegetables in the world, we will only be introducing those valued for their mystical properties. Before we do that, let's touch on the four classifications of vegetables:

### Root Vegetables

Root vegetables are the parts of the vegetables that grow underground. Most root vegetables are starches. Starch is a type of carbohydrate that the body uses for energy by turning it into glucose. Root vegetables have tons of fiber and antioxidants while being low in calories, fat, and cholesterol. However, if you consume more carbohydrates than your body needs, your body will store it away as fat, so it is recommended that you do not have more than one serving of root vegetables per day.

### Stem Vegetables

Stem Vegetables are the stalk or stem parts of the vegetable. Stem vegetables contain all the fiber, minerals and nutrients your body needs to run at full capacity. Adding too much fiber, especially if it wasn't already a regular part of your diet, can lead to gas and stomach cramping. It is recommended that you have no more than two servings of stem vegetables per day, though most do not include stem vegetables as part of a daily diet and opt for once or twice a week.

## Leafy Vegetables

Leafy Vegetables come from the leaf or leafstalk part of the vegetable. Leafy vegetables are considered the most important part of a healthy diet. Consuming leafy vegetables as part of your daily diet will assist in the fight against obesity, heart disease, and mental decline. For a boost in health and nutrition, aim for two cups of leafy vegetables per day.

## Bulb Vegetables

Bulb vegetables are the head or bulb part of the vegetable. They are important to help our body fight cancer, arthritis, and high blood sugar. Try for at least five serving of bulb vegetables per week, though there are no negative effects in consuming it every day or even more than once per day.

# Vegetables

A

**ARTICHOKE** (Cynara Cardunculus var. Scolymus)
**AKA** French Artichoke or Green Artichoke or Globe Artichoke
We remove the leaves and discard the choke. What we are left with is the heart of the artichoke. Artichokes are nutty and a little bitter in flavor. You can steam, boil, grill, braise, or stuff and bake artichoke. Easily flavored with basil, bay leaf, chervil, chives, coriander, mint, parsley, rosemary, sage, tarragon, or thyme

**Magical Uses**
Being the heart of the plant, it is no wonder that you would add artichoke to the meal when you are dealing with matters of the

heart, whether it be new love, seeking love, healing from a broken heart, or to strengthen the bond within a family or friendship.

**Healing Qualities**

Artichoke is great for liver health, blood pressure, and cholesterol.

**ASPARAGUS** (Asparagus Officinalis)

**AKA** Sperage or Prussian Asparagus or Sparagus or Sparrow Grass or Pru or Aspar Grass or Asper Grass or Spar Grass or Sparrows Guts

Fresh asparagus has no smell and the longer the spears, the more tender the taste. Eat raw as part of a salad, or steam, simmer, roast, toss in some batter, grill, sauté, or wok-fry. Flavors that go well with asparagus are chives, lemon balm, dill, garlic, and tarragon.

**Magical Uses**

Increase vigor, energy, sexual stamina, and potency in natural magic or inherited abilities. Consume before casting or summoning for added protection. Popular with those practicing sex magic, and consumed at least twenty minutes before ritual.

**Healing Qualities**

Asparagus is good for weight loss and is recommended for pregnant women.

B

**BUTTERBEAN** (Phaseolus Lunatus))

**AKA** Lima Bean or Sieva Bean or Double Bean or Madagascar Bean or Wax Bean

Smooth, creamy, and with a mild buttery flavor, butterbeans can be used in salads or added to meat or vegan curry.

**Magical Uses**

Butter beans are best used when you are going through periods of stress in your life. They will soothe the spirit as well as attract easier, less stressful times. Also good for cushioning feelings of loss, making them more manageable.

**Healing Qualities**

Rich in vitamins and minerals, butter beans are good for your general health.

## BEETROOT (Beta Vulgaris)

**AKA** Beet or Chard or European Sugar Beet or Red Garden Beet or Harvard Beet or Blood Turnip or Maangelwurzel Mangel or Spinach Beet

Beetroot smells and tastes like earth after a rainstorm. Turn it into a salad, boil, roast, add to your smoothie or slice thinly and bake until crisp and serve with dip.

**Magical Uses**

Attract love, prosperity and longevity with beetroot.

**Healing Qualities**

Beetroot helps with eye and liver health. It is also known to assist with blood pressure, and fight against strokes and heart disease.

## BELL PEPPERS (Capsicum Annuum)

AKA Sweet Peppers or Capsicum

This is where paprika comes from. Bell peppers are very sweet in taste. Add to salads or pan sear with sea food.

**Magical Uses**

Bell peppers will definitely ring the way to the bedroom.

Your dinner party will be as vibrant and sweet as the bell peppers being served, so prepare for an evening of easy and lighthearted fun.

Bell peppers will help someone struggling with shyness, but it needs to be eaten three times a week until desired effect has taken place.

**Healing Qualities**

Bell peppers are packed with vitamin A, fiber, and antioxidants. Bell peppers help protect against cardiovascular disease and certain cancers. Bell peppers help when it comes to flair-ups from inflammatory conditions, such as arthritis.

**BLACK-EYED PEAS** (Vigna Unguiculata)

**AKA** Goat Pea or Sothern Pea

Black-eyed peas have an earthy taste and should never have any odor. They work well with bacon, pork, or part of a vegetable stew.

**Magical Uses**

Black-eyed peas can increase the accuracy of psychic visions and make death stalking easier, when consumed beforehand.

**Healing Qualities**

Black-eyed peas are a great source of energy, and for improving nerve and muscle function.

**BROCCOLI** (Brassica Oleracea var. Italica)

**AKA** N/A

These florets give off a mild fresh taste. Add them to a stir fry or salad, or sauté or steam and use as part of a side dish or as a side dish on its own. No real need for anything more than a little salt and pepper for seasoning, but broccoli can be paired with basil, rosemary, oregano, or sage.

**Magical Uses**

Use broccoli for protection of what is yours or to attract prosperity.

## Healing Qualities

Broccoli contains cancer preventative compounds and is a good source of potassium. It is also good for high blood pressure, as well as heart, eye, and brain health.

## BRUSSELS SPROUTS (Brassica Oleracea var. Gemmifera)
### AKA N/A

The smaller the Brussels sprouts, the sweeter. The larger they are, the closer they get to cabbage in taste. Bake, simmer, or sauté to get the best flavor out of them. Season with basil, caraway, chives, cilantro or parsley.

### Magical Uses

Attract prosperity and peace by including Brussels sprouts in your meal.

### Healing Qualities

Brussels sprouts may protect against various cancers.

C

## CABBAGE (Brassica Oleracea var. Capitata)
### AKA N/A

Fair warning, the more you cook cabbage, the more it smells, and the smell itself is permeating. Cabbage comes in a variety of colors and tastes, from green and bitter to the purple that's slightly sweeter; from the red that's just a little peppery to the white that is sweet, mild, and earthy. Serve braised, sautéed, or turn into sauerkraut and serve with pork.

### Magical Uses

To celebrate a new relationship, baby, marriage, or new adoption, create one dish of each color, or one dish with all four varieties. Green cabbage will attract prosperity, purple cabbage will call upon the ancestors to bestow luck on future generations, red cabbage to make sure love stays abundant, and white to connect everyone on a spiritual level and seal the bond.

**Healing Qualities**

Eating cabbage can keep inflammation in check.

**CANARY BEANS** (Phaseolus Vulgaris)

**AKA** Mayocoba Beans or Peruano Beans

Buttery and mild in taste, these beans are a must in stews, soups, and curries. Otherwise, turn them into a summer dip for chips and freshly cut carrot sticks.

**Magical Uses**

Add canary beans to your dish before you endeavor on a new project of the creative variety, or to celebrate the completion of one, to ensure success. They also do well for happiness.

**Healing Qualities**

Canary beans are an excellent source of fiber, iron and calcium.

**CARROT** (Daucus Carota)

**AKA** N/A

Crunchy and almost fruity when raw, once cooked carrots are fluffy and have an earthy sweet flavor. From salads to side dishes, carrots are quite versatile when it comes to pairing them with other savory food.

**Magical Uses**

Carrots are good for increasing psychic awareness and the frequency of psychic visions, as well as improving their accuracy. It's also used to increase lust, energy, willpower, and for those suffering infidelity.

**Healing Qualities**

Carrots are a great source of Vitamin A. Besides psychic vision, carrots can help improve regular vision. It also regulates blood sugar, blood pressure, and weight management, lowers the risk of cancer, reduces the chances of heart disease while improving your immunity levels and boosting brain health.

# The Rabbit and the Sun

*Sitting outside cleaning and peeling carrots, my mother asked, "Did you know carrots are good for seeing?" I was almost six years old at the time a piped up, "That's why they don't need glasses!" She laughed and shook her head. "I said good for seeing, not for eyes..." And not for the first time, she proceeded to tell me this story.*

One day, the rabbit cried.

The sun, who was very fond of the rabbit asked, "Rabbit, for what reason do you cry? You are smart. You are fast. You are beautiful. There can be no reason for such tears."

The rabbit looked up at the sun and said, "Hyena mocks me. He laughs at me! Hunted by night and by day. My speed cannot protect me from the swift owl at night, or smart caracal, and especially the leopard who move quieter than a ghost."

"My dear rabbit, this is your place in the circle of life and death. And all of these are mighty animals, a death from them should be seen a privilege."

"And I am not worthy of them." Rabbit hung his head in shame. "For the hyena's mocking words were such: Even he and jackal, both who feed themselves off the scraps of others and trickery, they who are lazy, they can catch us. Even the vultures are known to pick us off from time to time."

The sun thought about this and said, "From my place in the sky, I can see all before it happens and what you say is true. As a speaker of chaos, I will try and help you. I will go to the moon, the speaker of balance, and together we come up with a plan."

The rabbit waited three days for the sun to return.

"The moon and I have spoken my dear rabbit." He said, "We cannot remove you from this circle of life and death, but I do have something to balance the odds."

Droplets of sunlight fell to the earth, so fast and hard that they went into the ground, buried beneath the soil.

"They will grow into food." The sun explained, "And when eaten it will grant the gift of sight, so that you may see the dangers ahead of you and swerve out of the mouth of death. Be warned that this is not unfailing, as to preserve the peace between chaos and fate."

The rabbit thanked the sun.

"This is not all, hyena will be punished for his mocking ways."

And so, the hyena was cursed to laugh, the sound quickly becoming familiar to rabbits and others who might fall prey to him, giving them a better chance to make an escape.

The drops of sunlight grew into food that we now call carrots, a gift of second sight from the sun.

**CAULIFLOWER** (Brassica Oleracea var. Botrytis)

**AKA** Cole Florye

Fairly nutty, almost sweet with a slight bitterness in taste. Eat raw, steamed, sautéed, or baked. The florets can be used to make a variety of side dishes, and go well with broccoli and if shredded, can make a wonderful alternative to rice.

Flavors that go well with it are almond, basil, bay leaf, cardamom, chervil, chives, coriander, cumin, dill, marjoram, mint, nutmeg, oregano, paprika, parsley, tarragon, thyme, and walnuts.

**Magical Uses**

If tempers are running high, or you expect them to, cauliflower will help soothe and calm them.

If you suffer from a short temper on a daily basis, add cauliflower to your meal twice a week to help increase levels of patience.

**Healing Qualities**

Cauliflower can aid in weight loss and indigestion. It is also said that it contains properties that fight certain cancers.

**CELERY** (Apium Graveolens)

**AKA** Dulce or Celeriac Root or Root Celery

Crunchy and bitter once cooked, celery adds a great earthy sweetness that should be used in soups and stews but should only be added two to five minutes before serving. For a sweet treat, fill it with peanut butter and raisins.

**Magical Uses**

Celery can help if there are communication problems between you and your partner. It can also aid in male virility.

When you have a fear that love is flickering into nonexistence, celery can help soothe those fears and strengthen bonds.

### Healing Qualities

Celery can help reduce inflammation and is good for digestion and high blood pressure.

## CHICKPEAS (Cicer Arietinum)

AKA Garbanzo Bean or Bengal Gram or Egyptian Pea

Raw or roasted, chickpeas have an earthy smell and nutty taste. The main ingredient of hummus, you can add chickpeas to salads, soups, stews, or eat them on their own as a healthy snack.

### Magical Uses

Add chickpeas to help protect you from, and to defeat, your enemies. From bullies to legal problems, chickpeas can help stack or sway the odds in your favor.

Chickpeas are also good for confidence issues, especially those suffering shyness because of previous abuse or bullying.

### Healing Qualities

Eat chickpeas for stronger bones and for a boost in mental health.

## CORN (Zea Mays)

AKA Maize or Mealie

Corn is both crunchy and sweet in taste. Boil, grill, remove from the cob and add to soups, salads, stews and stir fry. For a sweet side dish that goes well with savory and spicy meat dishes, try baking some corn bread.

### Magical Uses

Add corn to bring prosperity and protection to those attending your feast. It also encourages and strengthens bonds of love and friendship.

Corn is a great addition to harvest festivals and end of year celebrations, simply cook it with the pure intention of being grateful for everything good that happened and was received throughout the season. By showing gratitude, we attract another good season or year ahead.

**Healing Qualities**

Corn protects your cells against oxidative stress, and yellow corn is especially good for your eye health.

E

**EGGPLANT** (Solanum Melongena)

**AKA** Brinjal or Brinjal Eggplant or Aubergine

Eggplant smells fresh and earthy. When eaten raw, it is slightly bitter. When cooked, the taste becomes rich with a creamy texture. Try pairing eggplant with garlic, oregano, basil, thyme, rosemary, sage, or black pepper.

**Magical Uses**

Add eggplant to your meal for wisdom and insight, especially when dealing with matters of family or business.

If you are planning on some heavy spell work, whether on your own or as a coven, add a dish of eggplant to your pre-spell meal. If you are working as a group or coven, invite them to partake in the cooking ritual. Add purple eggplant for power and strength, and white eggplant for purification and protection. You may choose to use both, but then you should opt to create separate dishes for each.

**Healing Qualities**

Eggplant is great for weight loss and reduces the chances of heart disease.

F

**FAVA BEANS** (Vicia Faba)

**AKA** Broad Bean or Faba Bean or Boerbone

Fava beans are earthy, creamy, nutty and slightly sweet. Use fava beans in soups or side dishes. Flavor with parsley, rosemary, sage, thyme, garlic or onions.

**Magical Uses**

Consuming fava beans before spell casting will strengthen the outcome. Also add to meals regularly to increase power of spell casting capabilities.

**Healing Qualities**

Fava beans may help prevent birth defects.

G

**GREEN BEANS** (Phaseolus Vulgaris)

**AKA** String Beans or French Beans or Snap Beans or Haricots Verts

Green beans have a grassy taste and smell, they are great on their own or as part of a side dish. Pairs particularly well with bacon and potatoes.

**Magical Uses**

Consume green beans for prosperity earned through labor. Great for new jobs, projects or business ideas you know have potential.

There are times where you feel that your hard work is just not getting you anywhere, and green beans will help give you the motivation to continue on your journey.

**Healing Qualities**

Green beans are great for heart health.

H

**HORSERADISH** (Armoracia Rusticana)

**AKA** Khren or Hren or Ren or Red Cole

You will only discover the sharp earthy smell after grating or grinding horseradish. It is strong and spicy in flavor, and if you wish to avoid tears from the intensity of it you must remember to add white vinegar. It will still be spicy and pungent, so be careful if you have a delicate palate.

Add to sauces, mayonnaise, deviled eggs, potato salads, or to roast ham before it goes in the oven. Create a creamy sauce that is perfect for steak or rib or use horseradish to flavor any side dish of potatoes, beets, peas, broccoli, or leeks.

### Magical Uses

Experiencing a bit of bad luck? Then horseradish is a great addition. Try adding some to meals filled with intent of attracting good fortune.

Horseradish can make communicating with the ghosts of family members easier.

If you feel you or your family land is cursed, plant horseradish in every corner of the garden. Partake from whatever the plant produces, but only on the first day of every new moon. This will protect everyone within the borders from external or ancient curses. Do this until the plant dies.

Especially popular amongst newlywed couples trying to conceive. Add horseradish for male virility, increase sex drive, and fertility.

Horseradish is also used to rid negative spirits attached to you, or your bloodline through a curse or haunting. If you are using it for the latter, be sure to cook and eat horseradish once a month for nine months to be rid of the bloodline curse permanently.

### Healing Qualities

Horseradish is great for boosting metabolism and to clear up mucus or sinus issues. Filled with antioxidants and anti-bacterial qualities, horseradish can boost circulation and help protect against cell damage.

L

**LEEK** (Allium Porrum)

**AKA** Fake scallion

Leeks taste a bit like onion, only milder and sweeter, and you can use them the same way you would an onion. Bring flavor to stews, soups, quiches, meat dishes, or even uncooked as part of a salad. Thyme, tarragon, chives, garlic, mustard, and sage are flavors leeks pair well with.

**Magical Uses**

Leeks can provide a high level of purification and protection to those recently suffering from exorcism, and to prevent it from happening again. For this, consume once a week for three months.

Consume on the day of performing womanhood rituals. As a woman blooms, so does her magic. Leeks will help maintain the feminine magic within and shield it from the pollutants of the world until her naivety has worn.

**Healing Qualities**

Leeks may improve your digestion, assist with weight loss, reduce inflammation, fight heart disease, and combat certain cancers.

**LENTILS** (Lens Culinaris)

**AKA** N/A

Lentils come in a range of colors and are very easy to prepare. With a sweet earthy aroma, lentils taste a lot like beans when cooked properly. A very popular addition for curries and soups.

Pair lentils with woodsy herbs like sage, rosemary, and thyme.

**Magical Uses**

Expand your fortune by consuming a dish with lentils twice a week.

## Healing Qualities

Lentils are good for gut health, can lower cholesterol and blood pressure, protect against diabetes and lower the risk of colon cancer.

## **LETTUCE** (Lactuca Sativa)

**AKA** N/A

There are several types of lettuce, ranging in crunch and taste. You get dark leafed lettuce which includes Romaine, Green Leaf, Arugula and Butterhead; Iceberg lettuce which is also referred to as Crisphead lettuce; and a variety of red leafed lettuces including New Red Fire lettuce, Red Sails lettuce, Redina lettuce, Henry's Leafy Friend, Galactic lettuce, and Benito lettuce. Lettuce is mainly used in salads, sandwiches, and wraps.

## Magical Uses

The dark leafed lettuce is for abundance, iceberg for calming, and the red leafed for attracting employment, money, and prosperity.

## Healing Qualities

Lettuce has many anti-inflammatory properties.

O

## **ONION** (Allium Cepa)

**AKA** Bulb Onion or Common Onion

Fresh out of the soil, onion has no smell. From then, the smell, taste, and intensity depend purely on its age, ranging from sweet to tangy. Onions work well with a variety of meats, chicken, fish, or even on their own. They can be roasted, grilled, pickled, caramelized, battered, deep-fried, sliced thinly, or chopped and diced to be served raw in salads, sandwiches, dips, salsa, or as a garnish.

## Magical Uses

Red onion works well when you are trying to gain the affections of your dinner partner.

White onion helps to clear obstacles from your path, unless the obstacle is yourself in which case it will have no effect.

Purple onion is to be consumed if you are seeking to gain power, but it can also be used in meals intended to seduce.

Yellow onion, also known as brown onion, helps to dispel anger. Yellow onion is also good for spiritual healing and protection from dark spirits that may be following you.

**Healing Qualities**

Onion is an anti-inflammatory and has been linked to helping arthritis and bladder infections, as well as maintaining gut health.

P

**PARSNIP** (Pastinaca Sativa)

**AKA** N/A

Parsnips smell a bit like celery and have a sweet peppery taste. Parsnips are a must in chicken broths, soups, and in stews. They can also be baked, sautéed, steamed, mashed, pureed, and roasted. Flavor with rosemary, thyme, sage, and nutmeg.

**Magical Uses**

A meal that includes parsnips before centering will make energy harnessing a little easier. A meal including parsnip as part of your grounding ritual will help against those post casting jitters that can occur. Both meals can come from the same dish.

**Healing Qualities**

Parsnips have anti-fungal and anti-inflammatory properties.

**PEAS** (Pisum Sativum)

**AKA** Green Pea or Garden Peas

Peas have a fresh smell and a sweet or savory taste depending on the variety. There are a variety of recipes for peas as a side dish, and most of them are very simple and easy. Enhance their taste by pairing them with herbs and spices like mint, thyme, rosemary, dill, and black pepper.

**Magical Uses**

Add peas to a meal when you are trying to attract peace or prosperity into your life. Peas also work well to attract the perception of external beauty and love; but be careful that love found this way can be very fickle, and based around outward appearance or the perception of outward appearance.

**Healing Qualities**

Eating peas can help strengthen your immune system and lower cholesterol.

> *"Don't tell secrets or gossip in front of peas,"* my mother would say as she removed the peas from their pods. *"Else your words are bound to get out and reach the ears of everyone."*

## POTATO (Solanum Tuberosum)
**AKA** Tater or Spud

Earthy, nutty, and starchy, potatoes are one of the most eaten and popular vegetables in the world. Boiled, mashed, sliced, and fried, tossed alongside a roast or roasted on their own, the possibilities are truly endless. Same can be said about pairing them with other flavors! They are compatible with most spices, herbs, and edible flowers.

**Magical Uses**

If you are planning on performing sympathetic magic, also known as similarity or imitative magic, a dish with potatoes beforehand will help strengthen the outcome.

When infusing a potato dish for sympathetic magic, concentrate on the outcome of the sympathetic magic. Another option is to make crisps that can be eaten during the ceremony.

> *A magical tip for outside of the kitchen:*
>
> *Place a raw potato under the mattress, at the foot of the bed, to absorb nightmares. Each potato may be used for three days only. Then it must be buried in the garden, or deep in the compost heap, or burnt in an open fire until it is nothing more than ash.*

**Healing Qualities**

Rich in Vitamin C and high in potassium, potatoes can help prevent scurvy and aid in the health of our heart, muscle, and nervous system.

## PUMPKIN (Cucurbita)
**AKA** N/A

Pumpkin has a fruity aroma. Roasted pumpkin seeds make a delightful snack, especially when still warm, or as an interesting addition to salads and homemade breads. Pumpkin itself makes a wonderful and bright side dish whether roasted, steamed, or mashed. Serve as a sweet side dish covered in brown sugar and cinnamon, or as a fritter served with a caramel sauce.

**Magical Uses**

Serve pumpkin as a side dish when honoring the spirits or ancestors, to call upon protection from spirits, and to attract fertility or wealth.

Some people such as death stalkers, and those who have the gift of talking to, seeing, or feeling spirits, find it to be draining and even fearful. For those people, roasted pumpkin seeds will help. Keep them in an airtight container or Ziploc bag and nibble on a few as and when you need.

**Healing Qualities**

Boost your immune system and help protect your eyesight when you eat pumpkin. Also aids with sinus problems. Pumpkin seeds are a must have snack for those suffering high blood pressure.

R

**RADISH** (Raphanus Sativus)

**AKA** N/A

Crisp and zesty, with a spice factor that ranges from warm to mild. If your radishes have any odor, rather refrain from eating them, and it's best to put them at the bottom of the compost heap because the smell will increase while breaking down.

Radishes can be cooked but work best raw in salads and sandwiches. Place whole radishes, stem included, in iced water while you are preparing your other dishes. The iced water will keep them crisp. Radishes lose their potency when cut, so refrain from cutting and adding them to the meal till the very last minute.

### Magical Uses

Add red radish to your meal if you are in search of love. Add white radish to your meal if you are in need of spiritual protection.

### Healing Qualities

The nutrients found in radishes help lower blood pressure and can help reduce the risk of heart disease.

### RED KIDNEY BEAN (Phaseolus Vulgaris L.)

**AKA** Rajma or Common Kidney Bean

With a smokey and earthy taste, the red kidney bean is not to be confused with red beans which are small in size and differ in taste. They make a wonderful addition to hearty meals such as homemade chili, stews, soups, and curries, in both meaty and vegetarian based recipes.

### Magical Uses

Meals with red kidney beans should be served and eaten alongside those most dear to you, whether it be family, friends, or a coven. Such a meal would attract wisdom, love, and balance to everyone participating in the meal. You need not tell them, and see it as a secret gift you bestow on them.

Unless it's your coven, then you can choose to make a night out of creating the meal and enjoy its magical benefits together: The more energy infused into the meal, the stronger and better the outcome.

### Healing Qualities

Red kidney beans promote good colon health, are an excellent source of natural protein, and good for lowering cholesterol.

### RHUBARB (Rheum Rhabarbarum)

**AKA** Pie Plant

Fresh, fruity, sweet, reminiscent of berries, it is no surprise if you thought rhubarb was a fruit. While there is nothing quite like a rhubarb tart or pie, it can also be used to make a delightful jam to accompany roasted meats.

**Magical Uses**

Rhubarb jam is a wonderful magical gift, especially as a housewarming or baby shower gift because it attracts peace, protection, and happiness.

**Healing Qualities**

Rhubarb has anti-bacterial, anti-inflammatory, and anti-cancer properties.

**NOTE**: Rhubarb's heart shaped leaves are highly toxic. Discard them properly and wash your hands after.

S

**SCALLION** (Allium Fistulosum)

**AKA** Green Onion

Scallions taste a bit like onion, but with an undertone of fruitiness similar to apple. Eat them raw in a salad, or add to stir fry or stew, but if you do, add them last as they tend to wilt quickly in heat. To get the most out of the flavor, remember to slice scallions as thinly as possible.

**Magical Uses**

If you feel you words are being misunderstood, or that you struggle to communicate your feelings, adding scallions to your meal once a week can help with that.

Or you can add scallions to meals shared with family, friends, or simply a meal shared with someone you intend to have a serious conversation with. This will help with communication and to prevent misunderstandings.

**Healing Qualities**

Lower you risk of diabetes, heart disease, and cancer. Scallions also reduce inflammation have antioxidants that can lower cholesterol, boost immunity, and improve gut health.

## SPINACH (Spinacia Oleracea)
**AKA** N/A

Spinach must smell fresh. Any hint of mustiness, earthiness, bitterness, or sourness and it should go on the compost heap. When eaten fresh, it has a mild and slightly sweet taste, which becomes more robust when cooked. Chop it up finely and add to salads, soups, stews, and pasta dishes.

### Magical Uses

Cook with spinach if you are looking to attract good health. Eat meal with spinach before energy harnessing as it will provide a boost in energy and strength.

### Healing Qualities

Spinach helps against sinusitis, osteoporosis, and in strengthening the immune system. It is also helpful with regards to migraines, boosting hydration, and lowering blood pressure.

## SWEET POTATO (Ipomoea Batatas)
**AKA** Mislabeled Yams

Though it looks a lot like a yam, it's sweeter and less fibrous. Everyone loves sweet potato pie, fritters, and candied 'yams', but don't forget to pair it with rich pork and spicy dishes.

### Magical Uses

For those who have lost confidence and hope in themselves, their dreams, or aspirations, a dish of sweet potato is what is needed. To enhance the effect, serve with pork.

### Healing Qualities

Sweet potato enhances the immune system and brain function. It's good for eye-health, sinus, gut health, and has anti-cancer properties.

T

**TURNIP** (Brassica Rapa subsp. Rapa)

**AKA** Rutabaga or Swede Turnip or Swedish Turnip or Neep

Turnips have a woody smell that hovers between the smell of cabbage and that of a radish. Steam or boil and serve with butter and a dash of cream, add to soups, stews or throw in alongside a roast before you pop it in the oven.

**Magical Uses**

Add turnips to a meal before you perform a cleansing or a banishing to help make things go smoothly.

Turnips are also good if you are looking to remove obstacles from your life.

**Healing Qualities**

When eaten, turnips help protect us against harmful bacteria.

Y

**YAM** (Dioscorea)

**AKA** Amadumbe or Elephants Foot

Yams have a mild and earthy smell and are only slightly sweet. They tend to take on the taste of the spices and herbs they are cooked with. Eat them baked, mashed, candied, or in a cake, but if you want a real treat, cube and boil them in a little butter and lots of honey, cook until it is so soft that it has a consistency like mashed potatoes, and add a handful of marshmallows before serving.

**Magical Uses**

Eat yams as part of a summoning ritual, or to attract love.

## Healing Qualities

Include yams as part of your regular diet to boost brain health, reduce inflammation, and improve blood sugar control.

## Z

**ZUCCHINI** (Cucurbita Pepo)

**AKA** Courgette or Baby Marrow

Zucchini has a mild grassy aroma and tastes rather bland. Zucchini makes a wonderful side dish, especially for chicken, and you cannot go wrong with having zucchini bread on the table.

## Magical Uses

Add zucchini to your dish if you and your partner are having intimacy issues or have concerns about fidelity. Zucchini is also good for attracting prosperity.

## Healing Qualities

Zucchini may improve heart and vision health when consumed regularly.

# Fruit

## Mana

There are many names for it, but mana is a term to describe what our spirit is comprised of. Science calls it energy; it also resides inside every atom that makes up every cell in your body. Here is where it gets interesting: like everything else in the universe, our mana is in a state of constant vibration.

For that energy to be vibrating at a healthy and powerful frequency, in perfect harmony with the universe, one must also have a healthy body and a healthy mind where your spirit can thrive. There must be balance. The closer you are to achieving balance, the closer your frequency is to that of the universal frequency. This subsequently leads to stronger mana—the source of your magic— not to mention how much more alive and happier you will feel.

What does this have to do with fruit? Smoking, poor diet, medication, and pollution are just some of the things that put strain on your body at a cellular level. Science has labeled this as oxidative stress. The list of short-term effects is endless, ranging from lethargy to diabetes, and from digestive problems to cancer. Long term effects range from Parkinson's disease to Alzheimer's disease, and from multiple sclerosis to depression.

Raw fruits are not only nature's candy, but they are nature's tonic for all the terrible things we do to ourselves. By consuming as little as one piece of fruit, or cup of berries per day, you can increase your energy, help your body heal, and reverse the effects of oxidative stress on our cells. And unlike real candy—with the exception of bananas and raisins—you can pretty much have as much as you like per day. So, do not wait to infuse fruit in your magical dishes before consuming, but rather fill your activation bowl and include raw fruit in your daily diet if you desire to get the most out of your body and magic.

Fruit comes from trees, bushes, and vines. They can be eaten fresh, as part of a salad, stewed, bottled, baked, dried, and some even fried.

While there are hundreds of different fruits in the world, each good for your health, this book will only be focusing on those that have known magical properties.

## Fruits

A

**APPLE** (Pyrus Malus)
**AKA** N/A
One of the most common fruits in the world, they range from tart to sweet, crisp to almost creamy in texture. Use red apples for hot apple cider during the winter months. Firm red apples and bright green apples work well in tarts and pies. Chop up a green, gold, pink or any crisp apple, and add to a salad. If you are worried about browning, sprinkle with lemon juice. And if

you really have a sweet tooth or simply too many apples, candied apples or dried apple slices are always a winner.

## Magical Uses

- Cook and eat something made with red apples (twice a week for the best results), if you are seeking to attract love. It need not be romantic love, it could be the love found in friendship or family.
- Add gold apples to your meal to help with any plans you have to seek, or attract fame and popularity.
- Green apples work best if you are seeking prosperity and to brighten the future.
- Pink apples work to improve relationships.

---

*A magical tip for outside of the kitchen:*

*On occasion we could all use a little extra time. It could be for work projects, personal time, family gatherings, or events. For during those moments, cut an apple in half, sideways, not lengthwise, then remove all the pips and place them aside. You notice that the center looks like a five-pointed star. Cover the two halves in honey. Put the pieces back together and bind with a ribbon. All the while, concentrate on the time you need. Add the seeds to a fire, make sure nothing is left. Bury the ribbon bound apple, while having thoughts of gratitude for enough time.*

### Healing Qualities

Promote gut health, support weight loss, lower cholesterol, help fight asthma, and protect your brain when you regularly eat apples.

Eat green apples to sooth and cure a sore and itchy throat.

### APRICOT (Prunus Armeniaca)
### AKA N/A

Sweet and punchy, with a lush and sweet smell, apricots add a zing to any dish with pork chops or chicken. Use them when making scones, smoothies, and pies. They go well with dates, raisins, strawberries, and almonds. Have extra? Turn them into jam for a sweet treat or as a magical gift for someone else.

**Magical Uses**

Use apricots if you want to feel rejuvenated. Add to attract longevity and healing, during or after a sickness. Apricots can help attract love; turn your baked goods or jams into gentle love spells to heal and reunite a couple considering going separate ways despite the love they share.

**Healing Qualities**

Apricots promote eye health and help prevent heart disease.

**AVOCADO** (Persea Americana)

**AKA** Avo or Alligator Pear

Slightly sweet with a nutty aroma, avocado is a decent substitute for mayonnaise. You can use it in baking, as its own side dish, in guacamole, salads, and in a variety of vegan and pasta dishes.

**Magical Uses**

Partake in a dish with avocado before or during glamour, lust, and love spells to increase effectiveness.

**Healing Qualities**

Avocado can help reduce the risk of chronic disease as well as help lower cholesterol and lessen migraines. Avocado can also improve memory function.

B

**BAOBAB** (Musa)

**AKA** Monkey Fruit or Cream of Tartar Fruit

Dry, powdery, sweet with a sour, and sometimes bitter undertone, baobab fruit is best eaten straight from the shell, or sugar coated. If you have the powdered version, you can use it in baking, smoothies, and yogurt.

**Magical Uses**

Consume if you wish to commune with the spirits or improve death stalking abilities.

Good for longevity.

**Healing Qualities**

Baobab fruit can reduce fever and inflammation.

## BANANA (Musa)

**AKA** N/A

Soft, sweet, and delicious. Bananas work well as part of a dessert, pie, smoothie, or sliced over spicy curry with coconut flakes and chutney.

If your bananas start turning brown and are too squishy and bruised to eat, turn them into banana bread or muffins. A delightful treat and fun magical gift.

**Magical Uses**

Planning on traveling? Have some of those muffins, or buttered slices of banana bread before you go and take some on the journey for safe travels.

Banana is also good for increasing sexual stamina and fertility, as well as attracting prosperity.

**Healing Qualities**

Improve insulin sensitivity, blood sugar levels, and heart health with bananas. They also help with weight loss by making you feel fuller and providing great nutrients and potassium. This fiber rich fruit is also good for gut health, and gentle enough to eat on an upset stomach.

## BLACKBERRY (Rubus subg. Rubus)

**AKA** N/A

Floral in smell and tart in taste. Use blackberry in tarts, cakes, pavlovas, pancakes, cheesecakes, sauces for ice-cream, jams, and even sweet and savory glaze that goes fabulously with pork. Bottle in the form of jam or ice-cream sauces for later use.

**Magical Uses**

Blackberries can increase the sexual tension, bond, and increase passion in the bedroom. Do use sparingly, when used too often it can bring out the darker side of sex and passion.

Blackberries are also good for attracting health, wealth, and protection.

**Healing Qualities**

Boost brain and oral health when you add blackberries to your diet. Can also help in the fight against chronic sinus.

**BLUEBERRY** (Rubus subg. Rubus)

**AKA** N/A

Sweet, floral, and woody, you want to add blueberries to your waffles, pancakes, and smoothies. They work well in salads that have feta, walnuts, and spinach. Fabulous in jams and syrups.

**Magical Uses**

Strengthen your resolve or determination by adding blueberries to your meal. It can also brighten or strengthen your aura.

**Healing Qualities**

Blueberries are good for the heart, for bone strength, for skin health, blood pressure, diabetes, cancer prevention, sinusitis, and mental health.

C

**CANTALOUPE** (Cucumis melo var. cantalupensis)

**AKA** Rockmelon or Sweet Melon or Spanspek

Mild, sweet, and juicy, this fragrant fruit works well in fruit and green salads, as the main ingredient to sorbets and ice-cream, or combine with paprika as garnish for steak.

**Magical Uses**

Cantaloupe stimulates feelings of gratitude, attracts good energy, and helps with manifestation.

**Healing Qualities**

High in electrolytes and antioxidants. Cantaloupe is good for hydration and heart health.

**CHERRY** (Prunus Avium)

**AKA** N/A

There are hundreds of different cherries, each with its own distinct flavor, ranging from sweet to tart. When purchasing cherries, do a little research before putting them to use. Some are better in pies, tarts and baking. Others are good for snacking, salads and in chicken or pork dishes.

**Magical Uses**

Cherries attract happiness and love. If you are meeting new people, or have made a new friend, baked goods with cherries can help form or strengthen the bonds of new friendships.

**Healing Qualities**

Cherries have an impressive number of vitamins, minerals and nutrients, making it a powerhouse of goodness when eaten.

**CRANBERRY** (Vaccinium subg. Oxycoccus)

**AKA** Bearberry

These tart berries have an aroma similar to grapes. Eat them whole, add them to a salad, ice-cream, yogurt or smoothie. Or turn them into a jelly, jam or sauce that can be bottled and served with turkey or pork.

## Magical Uses

Bring people together, or help push those in toxic situations apart, with the help of cranberries.

## Healing Qualities

The juice is a perfect remedy for mild urinary tract infections. Cranberries also help prevent cavities, reduce inflammation, and help prevent certain cancers.

## COCONUT (Cocos Nucifera)
## AKA N/A

White and mildly sweet, coconut shavings give amazing texture and flavor, while coconut milk adds richness to the blandest of meals. Add the milk to curries and use the shavings as a garnish/topping for extremely warm curries to soothe the heat. The shavings can be used in baking and combine well with cocoa.

## Magical Uses

A dish with coconut can calm racing thoughts, and still a busy mind.

If you are feeling restless, unfulfilled and your thoughts about what to do muddled and confused, bake a batch of biscuits (or lamingtons) using either the milk or the shavings. While making the sweet treats, concentrate on being pointed in the right direction. Mull things over while snacking on one of the treats, you will find your thoughts a little clearer and your 'gut' a little louder. Continue doing this ritual twice a day until the batch is done. When you get to the last treat, concentrate on the actual options you have and make the choice that feels natural and right.

## Healing Qualities

Coconut is a good addition to a diet focused on bone health and is particularly good at protecting cells against oxidative stress.

## CUCUMER (Cucumis Sativus)
**AKA** Pickle

With a very mild scent and a sweet summery taste, cucumber is perfect for salads, sandwiches, and on burgers in place of lettuce. Add it to a jug of fresh water if you want a light summery drink to place on the table. Once pickled, they tend to have a sour and tangy taste and are called gherkins. Add gherkins to salads and sandwiches, in combination with the fresh cucumber, for that extra zing in flavor.

### Magical Uses

Add fresh cucumber to alleviate stress, calm the mind, and for mental rejuvenation. Use in conjunction with or before glamour, fertility, and lust spells. If you pickle cucumbers (turning them into gherkins), you can infuse them with the aforementioned magical qualities and uses. They store well as gherkins and make great magical gifts.

### Healing Qualities

Eating a cucumber is one of the easiest ways of hydrating. It also has vitamin A, which helps with bone health and blood clotting.

D

## DATE (Vaccinium subg. Oxycoccu)
**AKA** Dabino

Dates are sweet with an almost caramel taste, the level and intensity depending on which sort you purchase. Create a variety of syrups or sauces with dates, or simply add to them to your own red wine sauce recipe. Dates can be chopped up and added to salads and appetizers, and stuffing for chicken or turkey. Try your hand at baking cakes, tea loaves, or make a caramel sauce like no other.

### Magical Uses

Dates are wonderful for a psychic or mental rejuvenation and cleansing.

If you have a goal in mind, make a batch of date bars or biscuits while focusing on achieving your goals. Have one every morning and evening till they are finished, concentrating on the goals you have set, imagining what it will be like when you have completed them. This will help direct and focus your energy while diverting difficulties that stand in your path, so that you may pursue and achieve your goal.

**Healing Qualities**

There is evidence that suggests dates can induce labor and shorten the process of childbirth. It also promotes brain, bone, and gut health.

E

**ELDERBERRY** (Sambucus Nigra)

**AKA** Black Elder or European Elderberry or European Black Elderberry or Tramman

Earthy, tart and not overly sweet, it is perfect for adding to berry jams, fruity chutneys, syrups, tea, gin, or added to apple or berry pie filling.

**Magical Uses**

Use regularly should you feel the need for psychic protection or healing.

Serve elderberry tarts or elderberry jam on toast as part of a pre-summoning ritual for an added barrier of psychic protection, or serve during blessing ceremonies, including handfastings, baptisms, and initiations.

**Healing Qualities**

Elderberries can boost your immune system, help with sinus and inflammation, and protect your heart, as well as aiding with lessening stress levels.

F

**FIG** (Ficus Carica)

**AKA** N/A

With woody tones and creamy notes, its aroma is intoxicating, and its taste is sugary sweet. Turn figs into jams and chutneys, pies, tarts, and pastries. Add to salads and puddings. Serve with meats or cheese. The possibilities are quite endless, making figs easy to incorporate into cooking by those less familiar with the fruit.

**Magical Uses**

Figs can be used to attract peace, prosperity, and happiness.

Make fig bars or candied figs and gift them to a new bride or anyone trying to get pregnant. They should eat one every sunrise and sunset until finished. It promotes fertility, and grants protection over a future mother's womb.

If you are having trouble connecting to your feminine magic and feminine charm, bake a batch of fig cookies or biscuits. Eat one at midday for at least 9 days, preferably while sitting in the sun. While chewing on the biscuit, summon images of your perception of feminine grace, beauty, and power.

**Healing Qualities**

Improve bone density and in doing so help prevent osteoporosis when you add figs to your diet.

G

**GOOSEBERRY** (Ribes)

**AKA** Carberry or Dabberry or Dayberry or Dewberry or Fayberry or Feaberry or Fabes or Fapes or Feabs or Feaps or Goggle Berry or Goosegog or Goosegob or Groser or Groset or Grizzle berry or Honey-blob or Wineberry

Once ripened, they have a sourness, but it is mixed in with a sweet melon sort of flavor. Gooseberries make fine tarts, jams, and chutney, or as part of the mix for chicken stuffing.

**Magical Uses**

Eat a dish with gooseberries before or while performing illusion magic or glamour magic, to lengthen the spells half-life.

Or you can combine a gooseberry dish with an invocation ritual to strengthen. Serve gooseberry tartlets, or gooseberry jam on toast, to everyone involved at the beginning and end of the ceremony.

They are also good for calling adventure.

**Healing Qualities**

High in fiber, low in calories, rich in antioxidants, protects brain health, good for your heart, and has anti-cancer effects.

**GRAPEFRUIT** (Citrus × Paradisi)

**AKA** Pomelo or the Forbidden Fruit

Grapefruit may have an exotic sweet smell but are extremely bitter tasting. That does not mean it cannot be used in the kitchen. With the help of sugar and natural sweeteners, like honey, grapefruit can make the most delicious summer tarts, puddings, and fruit juices. Grapefruit can be a wonderful addition to a salad. If you are making a garden salad, you can pair with almonds, basil, cashews, cumin, mint, parsley, rosemary, thyme, avocado, or spinach. For a fruit salad, it can be used in combination with cherry, coconut, orange, pineapple, pomegranate, or raspberries.

**Magical Uses**

For a boost in confidence or self-esteem, grapefruit is both helpful and uplifting when used. Consume daily to protect your emotional well-being if you feel under constant threat of the Evil Eye.

**Healing Qualities**

Grapefruit is high in vitamin c, helping fight bacteria, and supporting the immune system, as well as aiding in weight loss and lowing blood pressure.

## GRAPES (Vitis)
**AKA** N/A

Different grapes have different smells and tastes, ranging from musty to sweet. Grapes make wonderful jams and give salad dressings a unique taste. They can also be part of a salad or fruit kebab.

### Magical Uses

Grapes in general are perfect for attracting abundance.

Green grapes attract prosperity.

Use purple grapes if you are wanting to increase your psychic abilities and to strengthen your magic.

Red grapes work best for attracting love, increasing lust, and for fertility.

**NOTE:** Raisins are tricky. Raisins are made by drying grapes, ultimately turning them a shade of brown. So, unless you know what color grape was used to make a specific raisin, rather use raisins for attracting abundance. Besides being a fun addition to dishes like bobotie and yellow rice, you can incorporate them into a snack pack with seeds and nuts before placing the pack in your activation bowl for a day or two.

### Healing Qualities

Improve memory, attention, and mood when you include grapes in your diet. They are also known to improve heart, eye, and bone health, as well as in lowering blood sugar levels and cholesterol.

## GUAVA (Psidium Guajava)

**AKA** N/A

Guava has a sweet and musky smell, and its subtle flavor is something between a strawberry and a pear. Use guava in cheesecakes or tarts. Or simply turn it into an incredibly fruit juice that can be mistaken for syrup because it is so thick and can be thinned out with apple juice. This fruit is also delicious if you dehydrate them.

**Magical Uses**

Create guava tartelettes, mini cheesecakes, or serve as homemade dried fruits during fertility and sex rituals. Speaking of sex, a dessert with guava is a fantastic way to end a romantic dinner when you want the evening to end in passionate sex."

Guava can also be used to attract wealth, or to replace drained creativity.

**Healing Qualities**

Guava helps to relieve the painful symptoms of menstruation. It is also good for heart health and promotes good skin.

H

**HONEYDEW** (Cucumis Melo L.)

**AKA** Bailan Melons

Sweet and with a very subtle flavor, honeydew pairs well with certain fish, and can be made into a refreshing sorbet or a summer drink.

**Magical Uses**

Honeydew should be served at weddings to encourage eternal love and a successful marriage. Serve during courtship to encourage true love and if you are wishing for a hasty engagement. If the love is predicted to be unhealthy for either party, the honeydew will in turn work at keeping each party safe and sending them on separate paths as soon as possible.

**Healing Qualities**

Reduce blood pressure, stabilize blood sugar, and promote bone health when you include honeydew in your diet.

K
## KIWI (Actinidia)
**AKA** Chinese Gooseberry

Citrusy and sweet, kiwi works well in salads, salsas, and chutney. During hot summer months try baking some kiwi bread to go with that barbeque, or make refreshing ice cream, sorbets, and smoothies. Kiwi goes well with strawberries.

### Magical Uses

Reinvigorate your sex and love life with kiwi dishes. It can also be used to attract prosperity or success.

If you are trying to be charming and attract attention, kiwi at sunrise, midday, and sunset are sure to do the trick. Homemade dehydrated kiwi pieces kept in an airtight container is a convenient way to have on hand when you need.

### Healing Qualities

Support heart and digestive health, as well as boost your immune system when you include kiwi in your diet. Also, kiwi is good if you suffer chronic sinusitis.

## KUMQUAT (Fortunella)
**AKA** Cumquats

Sour, tangy, and slightly sweet, the best part about this citrusy fruit is its sweet tasting peel. Use kumquats in jams, chutney, stuffing, or bake it into breads, cakes, cookies, or pies.

### Magical Uses

A magical gift containing kumquat, brings prosperity to those receiving the gift. Usually gifted at the beginning of a new season or year, to celebrate harvests, or any occasion the family exchanges gifts like birthdays or anniversaries.

Consume before performing defensive magic for stronger outcome.

**Healing Qualities**

Kumquats help protect your cells from damage and oxidative stress. They provide a boost of vitamin C during flu season, and they promote bone, heart, and skin health.

L

**LEMON** (Citrus Limon)

**AKA** N/A

Citrus in smell and sour in taste, lemons have the ability to make your mouth water just by thinking about them. Lemons give amazing flavor to baked goods, sauces, salad dressings, marinades, drinks, and desserts. Do not shy away from using lemon to flavor chicken or fish.

**Magical Uses**

Lemon can attract longevity.

Serve a dish or baked goods made with lemon before, or during and as part of, love and beauty spells to enhance their strength. Or simply infuse the dish or beverage with love and beauty and consume as a mini ritual for both. Before the taste of the last bite fades from your mouth, take a good look at your reflection before telling yourself that you are beautiful and worthy of love. You can do this every third day until you feel both beautiful and know your true worth.

**Healing Qualities**

Lemons aids in lowering blood pressure and weight loss. It also reduces the risk of heart disease, anemia, kidney stones, digestive issues, and certain types of cancer.

Simply add to your daily drinking water but be sure to not overdo it as lemons are highly acidic and too much could temporarily irritate the stomach.

## LIME (Citrus × Aurantiifolia)
**AKA** N/A

Lime has a citrusy candy smell and a pleasant albeit extremely tart taste. Use the rind to flavor drinks, marmalades and jams, sorbet, chutney, pickles, salad dressing, and desserts. The juice of the lime makes for summery and refreshing taste in tarts and cocktails. A splash of lime juice can enhance the tastes of risottos, fish, and chicken dishes.

**Magical Uses**

Use lime to induce lust, jealousy, and release inhibitions.

It can also be used for healing and protection.

**Healing Qualities**

Lime can reduce inflammation and help prevent a list of chronic illnesses.

## LYCHEE (Litchi Chinensis)
**AKA** Litchi or Lichi or Alligator Strawberry

The white flesh of the sweet lychee makes for an amazing juice or a fun addition to punch bowls and fruit salad, or add to chicken and rice dishes.

**Magical Uses**

Use lychees to attract happiness and sweetness in day-to-day life. If can be used in conjunction with beauty spells and before divination for stronger more accurate effects.

Lychees also give the eater energy and motivation.

Use to grant wishes. Concentrate on what it is you desire while you prepare your dish, and while eating, concentrate on being thankful as well as imagine the wish already being granted. Imagine the feeling you will experience when the wish comes true.

**Healing Qualities**

Lychee helps improve bone and heart health, but also protects the body at a cellular level from oxidative stress.

M

## MANDARIN ORANGE (Citrus Reticulata)

**AKA** Clementine

Mandarin oranges are tropical and citrus in taste and smell. Usually used in salads, marmalades, and liqueurs but can add a fruity aroma when added to duck or chicken.

**Magical Uses**

Include some mandarin when hosting a dinner party to encourage cheerfulness and friendships. Mandarin is also good when you are struggling to unwind and need a calming influence.

**Healing Qualities**

Add mandarin oranges to a child's diet to encourage normal growth and physical development. Mandarin is also good for your immune system and eyesight.

## MANGO (Mangifera Indica)

**AKA** Love Fruit or Queen Fruit

Mango is juicy, sweet with a taste that balances between citrus and melon. Cube or slice and add to salads, smoothies, curries, and pavlova. Bring a tropical feel to summer gatherings and barbeques by using mango to create fluffy mousse and cheesecakes, or refreshing fridge tarts, ice-creams, or sorbet.

**Magical Uses**

A dish with mango was traditionally brought with to orgies to encourage sex and love. While this is still an option, there are modern ways to use this fruit. For example, if you are hosting or bringing a dish to a valentine's party, or to serve as part of a courtship or romantic meal. Mango dishes can be served at weddings and anniversary dinners. For best effects, serve at the end of the meal, or as part of dessert.

If you are part of a predominantly female coven (or even just a group of girlfriends), sharing a mango dish is a wonderful way to connect on a deeper level, both emotionally and magically.

If you are doing it to bond at a magical level and really want to tap into the collective feminine energy, do this during the first night of the full moon. This will also enhance any magicks you or your coven perform for the remaining two nights of full moon.

**Healing Qualities**

Mango supports heart, digestive and eye health, and has immune boosting nutrients.

# MULBERRY (Morus Alba)

**AKA** N/A

Sweet, tart, and tangier than blackberries, mulberries add great flavor to smoothies, milkshakes, ice-cream or added to salads, yogurts or custard dishes, or turn into jams and sauces.

**Magical Uses**

Mulberries are good for increased magical awareness, encouraging quality premonitions and enhancing precognitive abilities.

**Healing Qualities**

At the beginning of this chapter, there was mention made about the damage done daily to our bodies called oxidative stress. Mulberries are phenomenally good at reversing this damage at cellular level.

# MUSKMELON (Cucumis melo)

**AKA** Melon or Sweet Melon.

Muskmelon can be either sweet or bland, it works well in smoothies, as part of a fruit salad or fruit and granola medley. Or drape thinly sliced Italian ham (also known as Prosciutto) over wedges of muskmelon, and voila! An instant amuse-bouche.

**Magical Uses**

Muskmelon stimulates feelings of gratitude, attracts good energy, and aids with manifestation.

**Healing Qualities**

Muskmelon is an easy way to keep hydrated because of its high-water content. It also acts as an immune booster, is good for vision and cardiovascular health. Muskmelon aids in weight loss and can help combat stress.

N

**NAARTJIE** (Prunus Avium)

**AKA** Miyagawa Mandarin or Unshu Mikan or Cold Hardy Mandarin or Satsuma Mandarin or Satsuma Orange or False Tangerine

(Pronounced *Gnar-chee*) Small, round, and easy to peel, naartjies taste like a cross between and orange and a mandarin, but slightly sweeter. Use them in salads, or to flavor baked goods like cakes and koeksisters.

**Magical Uses**

Consume a dish with naartjie one hour before attempting to communicate with a negative, restless or aggressive spirit. Your words will be soothing and create a sense of calmness to the spirit.

**Healing Qualities**

Consume regularly for healthy glowing skin. The terpenes released during the pealing process is good for anxiety and depression.

O

**OLIVE** (Olea Europaea)

**AKA** N/A

Raw and good quality olives are usually bitter. Cure in water for a week to remove the bitterness and release the fresh nutty flavor, then store and bottle in brine. They can then be added to salads or sliced and sprinkled over pizza. Serve olives instead of nuts when drinking alcohol as it will line the stomach and helps to prevent a hangover.

**Magical Uses**

Store bought bottled olives will work if you place the bottle in your activation bowl, but not nearly as well as the home-made variety. While olives take several days before you can eat them, the energy and intent you infuse into them during times of preparation, increases, and strengthens during the curing and pickling process.

Olives attract wisdom, longevity, prosperity, and peace.

**Healing Qualities**

Olives reduce the risk of cancer, diabetes, strokes, and heart disease.

**ORANGE** (Citrus × Sinensis)

**AKA** N/A

Sweet, citrus, and almost exotic, oranges are bright in not only smell and taste, but in color too. Oranges can be used when cooking beef, chicken, or veal dishes. The flesh and rind make amazing marmalades, chutneys, and salad dressings. Oranges add a delicate flavor to breads and a zest to tarts, cheesecakes, mousse, and citrus bars.

**Magical Uses**

Use orange if you find yourself drained of motivation, passion, and creativity. Consume as often as you need.

Oranges can also be used to attract romance and love.

**Healing Qualities**

Oranges help the body produce collagen and help to improve skin tone and quality. Also good for high blood pressure.

**PAPAYA** (Carica Papaya)

**AKA** Pawpaw or Papaw

Sweet with a melon taste and a smooth creamy texture, papaya can be used in curries, dips, and to tenderize meat. On the sweeter side, papaya makes for creamy shakes, smoothies, or desserts.

**Magical Uses**

Papaya can be used to increase the quality and quantity of sex, love, and lust shared in a relationship.

Papaya can also be used to attract wealth in the form of knowledge and, or riches, making it perfect for consumption before new jobs, studies, or projects.

**Healing Qualities**

Papaya has anti-cancer properties, will improve heart health, fight inflammation, and sinusitis, improve digestion and help protect the skin against damage caused by the sun and pollution.

**PASSIONFRUIT** (Passiflora Edulis)

**AKA** Grenadine or Passionflower or Purple Granadilla or Purple Passion Fruit.

Passionfruit is tart, sweet, and juicy when you bite into it. Use passionfruit to create summer puddings, ice-creams, smoothies, fruit juice, and cheesecakes.

**Magical Uses**

Serve a dish of passionfruit to someone seeking to conceive a baby, or one that is already with child. It will help with fertility, and to protect the mother.

**Healing Qualities**

Passionfruit not only provides key nutrients and antioxidants, but it supports heart health and can reduce anxiety when consumed often.

**PEACH** (Prunus Persica)

**AKA** N/A

Sweet and gentle in taste, like custard, peaches have a vanilla honey smell. Peaches make wonderful chutney and stewed or bottled fruit. Add them to warm curries, and spicy dishes of pork or chicken. Bottled peaches make for a wonderful last-minute desert that can be served with vanilla ice-cream or kept as an easy-to-grab magical gift. Either way, bottled peaches won't stay on the shelf for too long. Get creative by adding peaches to tartlets, trifles, cobbler, other crumbed desserts, or baked on its own and stuffed with cookie and topped with cream.

**Magical Uses**

Peaches attract fidelity, happiness, longevity, and love, as well as grant general protection and protection from spirits.

**Healing Qualities**

Peaches are known to offer protection from lung and oral cancers.

**PEAR** (Pyrus)

**AKA** N/A

Sweet across the board, pears range in firmness, from being crisp, to having the texture of partially crystalized honey. You can add pear to garden or chicken salad, or with pork chops. For an after-dinner treat, add pear to tea bread, tarts, or a variety of warm desserts.

**Magical Uses**

Use pear to attract health, longevity, wisdom, or protection.

Share a pear inspired dish with someone if you are trying to encourage lust or love. A dish like this cannot force love or lust, it can only stimulate whatever hidden feelings there are beneath the surface.

**Healing Qualities**

Pears have been linked to lowering the risk of diabetes. They also work as an anti-inflammatory, and aid in gut health and weight loss.

**PERSIMMON** (Diospyros Kaki)

**AKA** N/A

With their mild honey taste, persimmons make a delightful jam. You can also use them in risottos and bake into breads or cookies.

**Magical Uses**

Persimmons help if you are struggling with yourself or your identity. During difficult times, have persimmon jam on toast or a persimmon cookie every day at sunrise and sunset. It will help ease your panic and suffering, as well as attract better times to come faster.

**Healing Qualities**

Persimmons are a regular must for those suffering with anemia, or for those who bruise easily. Persimmons can also reduce the chance of strokes and certain cancers.

**PINEAPPLE** (Ananas Comosus)

**AKA** N/A

Tropical and mouthwatering, pineapple ranges from surgery sweet to extremely tart. From juice to sorbets, tarts to cakes, fruit to garden salad, your options for using pineapple in the kitchen is endless.

Pineapple is the only fruit that eats you while you eat it, which is why your tongue starts to sting if you eat too much over a short time. For this reason, allow beef, pork, or ham to soak in pineapple juice for twelve to twenty-four hours before the time; it not only provides great flavor but will make the softest juiciest meat you have ever had.

**Magical Uses**

Pineapple brings luck and prosperity, but there is a catch if you want it for yourself. A dish or meal with pineapple must be served to a group of people, usually family or friends. Your intention, while cooking and serving, is to bestow luck and prosperity on them and them alone. If the winds of luck so wish it, you will receive your even share. Either way, selfless magic tends to be good for magical kismet and karma.

To negate this and make it more potent, you can work as a coven in creating and serving the dish. Another way is to use the fresh pineapple juice technique mentioned above. You will need to do the opening and closing ceremony once: when you make the juice and prepare your meat for its soak. The longer you soak the meat, the more potent the magic becomes. Do remember to store in the refrigerator.

If you choose, you can do a second opening and closing ceremony when cooking the meat, but this is really only necessary if you are creating magical side dishes and accompaniments.

**Healing Qualities**

Pineapple is good for sinus sufferers, as well as having anti-inflammatory, and pain killing properties.

**PLUMS** (Prunus Domestica)

**AKA** N/A

Plums have a very subtle aroma until baked, then they release a fruity almost cinnamon aroma. In taste they vary from sweet to tart. Plums can be used to make jams, chutneys, crumbles, and tarts. But get the most out of this fruit when used to create a sauce for chicken, steak and pork dishes.

**Magical Uses**

Try a plum dish before or as part of a beauty and love spell, or before a summoning for protection and clear wits.

If you are shy by nature, or have a problem with spontaneity, plums will help you with that. You will however need to dry them out in the oven or a food dehydrator, turning them into prunes. Long lasting and easy to carry around in this form, you can simply pop one in your mouth when you need.

**Healing Qualities**

Adding plums to your diet can help lower the risk of heart disease. Plums can help with daily anxiety, constipation, high blood pressure, and bone health.

## POMEGRANATE (Punica Granatum)
**AKA** N/A

Fruity, floral, and sweet, pomegranate seeds are great in green salads with feta, spritzers, summer chicken dishes, and baked chocolate goods.

**Magical Uses**

Make a wish on a dish with pomegranate, or consume for luck, wealth, and as part of a fertility ritual.

Combine cocoa and pomegranate, to get a dish that will help you catch the lustful eye of someone. This is good if you are looking for a purely sexual connection.

**Healing Qualities**

Pomegranate helps to prevent and treat several types of cancer, as well as cardiovascular disease, osteoarthritis and rheumatoid arthritis. It helps wounds to heal faster and is very beneficial to the reproductive system.

## PRICKLY PEAR (Opuntia)

**AKA** Indian fig or Mission Cactus or Barbary Fig or Cactus Pear or Paddle Cactus

Soft and sweet and juicy, with a taste reminiscent of sweet melon, prickly pears make incredible jams, chutneys, or a syrup that must be tried with pork ribs, roast, or tenderloin recipes.

### Magical Uses

Call upon hope and endurance for tough times ahead.

Prickly pear can assist those struggling to adapt to new circumstances or situations.

### Healing Qualities

Prickly pears can aid those with diabetes, high cholesterol, obesity, and is the perfect cure for hangovers. It's also known for its anti-inflammatory properties.

## Q

## QUINCE (Cydonia Oblonga)

**AKA** N/A

Though it looks juicy and sweet, the quince is actually dry and sour. This is the only fruit you must cook if you want to enjoy it. Once cooked it changes color and becomes more tangy than sour with a hint of sweetness. It works great in jams and jellies, but what you really want to use it for is to flavor chicken.

### Magical Uses

Quince will help heal a broken heart, bring happiness, and possibly new love. This magic generally works better when a coven come together to make it, and share it, and in doing so share in the pain and hasten the healing process.

### Healing Qualities

Quince can help manage pregnancy-induced nausea. It is also good for digestive issues, treat stomach ulcers, and acid reflux symptoms.

## R
**RASPBERRY** (Rubus Idaeus)

**AKA** N/A

Juicy with hints of floral and woody tones, raspberry makes delightful tarts and jams. Add raspberries to pork, venison, and other game meats.

**Magical Uses**

Raspberries encourage kindness to grow within you, and to encourage it within those you meet and interact with.

**Healing Qualities**

Raspberries help improve heart function and lower the risk of getting a stroke. It also contains properties that benefit bone and skin health. They can aid those who suffer high blood pressure.

## S
**STRAWBERRY** (Fragaria × Ananassa)

**AKA** Garden Strawberry

Juicy and ranging from sweet to tart, strawberries can be used in a variety of tarts, salads, desserts, and drinks. Turn them into fruit juice or jam, or try adding them to pork dishes.

**Magical Uses**

Share a dish made with strawberries with your partner to protect your relationship from infidelity and to increase feelings of love. Strawberries are also very good at encouraging an atmosphere of attracting love and luck.

**Healing Qualities**

Adding strawberries to your regular diet will help reduce the risk of cancer, diabetes, strokes, and heart disease, as well as lower cholesterol and blood pressure.

**TIP**: Store strawberries in an airtight glass jar, inside your refrigerator. This will help them keep fresh far longer than expected.

T

**TANGERINE** (Citrus Reticulata)

**AKA** N/A

You cannot go wrong when you add this super zesty fruit to marmalade, baked goods, salads, or chicken. If your recipe calls for mandarin, you can always interchange it with tangerine without compromising on taste or texture.

**Magical Uses**

Serve tangerine dishes before or as part of a cleansing ceremony to help banish negative energies and spirits, and to prevent them from returning. If you are worried the spirits will attach themselves to the house instead, scatter the tangerine peels over the table before feasting on the dish you made.

**Healing Qualities**

Support brain health and get clear youthful skin when you add tangerine to your regular diet.

**TOMATO** (Solanum Lycopersicum)

**AKA** Love Apple

Tomatoes range in color, size, juiciness, flavor, and level of sweetness. They can be used in too many ways to mention, from sauce to soup to salad, they work well with meat, fish or poultry, and vegan or vegetarian dishes.

**Magical Uses**

Tomatoes are usually used to attract, encourage and help with love, seduction, passion, but they work well to remove curses.

**Healing Qualities**

Adding tomatoes to your regular diet can help reduce blood pressure and severely reduce your chances of having a stroke.

W

**WATERMELON** (Citrullus Lanatus)

**AKA** N/A

Sweet and fresh smelling, watermelon goes well with feta cheese to make a light summer salad, or to make sorbets, popsicles, and delicious fruit drinks.

**Magical Uses**

A dish of watermelon will reinvigorate the spirit and help restore mana lost during energy harnessing and spell casting. For protection and guidance, eat before communing with nature spirits. Can also be used as part of, and to intensify, beauty and glamour spells.

**Healing Qualities**

Watermelon is good for clear skin, inflammation, and healing your body at a cellular level, reversing the damage from oxidative stress.

Cassandra Sage

# Nuts

## The Power of Nuts

A nut is just a fruit with a hard protective exterior. Unlike seeds, nuts don't open naturally or release their contents.

Great for the heart and packed with nutrients and healthy fats, do you need another reason to add nuts to your diet? Just beware not to overdo them as they are high in calories.

When it come to their place in kitchen magic, nuts in general are associated with inner truth, strength, protection, and wisdom, but most also have their own unique magical quality.

All edible nuts have the ability to make energy harnessing easier, and to quicken the outcome of spell casting, manifestation rituals, and sympathy magic. But you do not need to add them to your meals to achieve the outcome. Without removing the shells, simply place the nuts in your activation bowl, and speak your words of intent. Leave untouched for at least one day. Then consume a few before energy harnessing for effect.

Besides bowl activation, nuts can be used to create some nutty magical dishes.

Cassandra Sage

**ALMONDS** (Prunus Dulcis)

**AKA** N/A

Use almonds in baking, chicken dishes, casseroles, and dips.

**Magical Uses**

Almonds bring love.

**Healing Qualities**

Almonds help with migraines, blood sugar control, gut health, and unstable blood pressure and in lowering cholesterol levels.

**BRAZIL NUT** (Bertholletia Excelsa)

**AKA** N/A

This nut pairs very well with chocolate and is generally crushed and used to give flavor and crunch to brownies, cakes, and cheesecakes.

**Magical Uses**

Increase lust and passion with these nuts. Not just for another person, but for life.

**Healing Qualities**

Brazil nuts will help reduce inflammation, support brain function, improve thyroid function, and improve heart health.

**CASHEW** (Anacardium Occidentale)

**AKA** N/A

Add cashews to stir fry or salads.

**Magical Uses**

Cashews help you to become lucky in love.

**Healing Qualities**

Cashews can help prevent heart disease, and are good for brain and bone health.

**CHESTNUT** (Castanea Sativa)

**AKA** N/A

Chestnuts can be candied, roasted, added to soups, and with pork dishes.

**Magical Uses**

Chestnuts can help you on your path to gaining wisdom by helping you retain knowledge, improve judgement and your other natural instincts.

**Healing Qualities**

Adding chestnuts to your diet can help prevent diabetes and boost the immune system, increase bone mineral density, relieve digestive problems and improve cognitive functions.

**HAZEL** (Corylus)

**AKA** Hazelnut or Filbert or Cobnut

Hazel is most commonly used in baking, desserts or chocolate.

**Magical Uses**

This is another nut used to gather wisdom, by helping you understand and empathize better with people and animals.

Hazel nuts can also help you to communicate with local nature spirits, including the Fae. It allows the spirits to better understand our words and the intentions behind them, but do not try be dishonest or hide your true intentions for they will know.

**Healing Qualities**

Hazel nuts can help decrease blood fat levels, regulate blood pressure, reduce inflammation, and improve blood sugar levels.

**PEANUT** (Arachis Hypogaea)

**AKA** Ground Nut or Monkey Nut or Goober

Use crushed peanuts in salads, cookies, sauces, or made into peanut butter.

**Magical Uses**

Peanuts can help prevent poverty.

**Healing Qualities**

Peanuts can help lower cholesterol.

**PECAN** (Carya Illinoinensis)

**AKA** N/A

Pecans can be used in a variety of pies, or sprinkle over a green salad or banana split .

**Magical Uses**

Pecan nuts attract prosperity.
### Healing Qualities
Pecan nuts can help to lower blood pressure.

### PINE (Pinus Pinea)
### AKA N/A
Pine nuts can be used in pesto sauce, sandwiches, cakes, bread, salads, pizzas, and biscuits.
### Magical Uses
A dish of pine nuts can help increase levels of lust between the two sharing it.
### Healing Qualities
Pine nuts help keep your skin in good condition and youthful looking.

### PISTACHIO (Pistacia Vera)
### AKA N/A
Pistachio is used in sauces, dips, ice cream, cake, truffles, and pastries.
### Magical Uses
Pistachio attracts new love and can help increase love that is already there.
### Healing Qualities
Pistachios as part of a regular diet can help regulate blood sugar, blood pressure, and cholesterol levels.

### WALNUT (Juglans)
### AKA N/A
Add walnuts to desserts, seafood pasta, or taco meat.

**Magical Uses**

Consume walnuts to attract prosperity and employment.

**Healing Qualities**

Walnuts are good for brain health and in preventing certain cancers.

# Mushrooms
## The Fun in Fungi

While there are countless mushrooms in the world, not all of them are edible. They are not considered to be plant or animal and are classified as fungi. And fungi feed us more than we realize: bread, chocolate, cheese, soy sauce, beer, and wine as we know it, not to mention an array of medicines that could not have come into being without the involvement of fungi.

They are also the unsung heroes, warriors protecting our climate by breaking down toxins in the ground and dealing with carbons responsible for carbon-dioxide. But it is not just the planet it is looking out for...

Unlike fruit that heals us at a cellular level (as mentioned in chapter three), consuming mushrooms regularly will protect those very cells, keeping them safe and free from damage, helping to keep your inner frequency in tune with the universe.

Cassandra Sage

### Musical Mushrooms:

*My mother was an avid gardener, everything from flowers to vegetables, but her pride and joy was her mushroom garden.*

*Whenever it came time to harvest, we would sit under the tree, her removing spores and me cleaning the mushrooms with a soft cloth. And we would always sing as we went about our work. The only rule being that we could not stop until the task was done. I asked her about it one day.*

*"They are alive," she said, "Mushrooms sing along to the frequency of the universe."*

*And she told me that when we sing, the mushrooms will adjust their tune, working to harmonize between the universal frequency and the song. And when we eat those mushrooms, we consume that harmony and find ourselves more attuned to the earth, the universe, and the natural flow and ebb of magic that connects us all.*

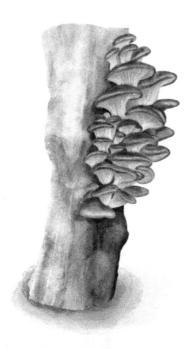

## Mushrooms

**BUTTON MUSHROOM** (Agaricus Bisporus)

**AKA** White Button Mushroom or White Mushroom or Common Mushroom or Champignon or Table Mushroom

Use button mushrooms in pasta dishes, stir fry, omelets, salads, soups, sauces, roasts, or part of a topping for pizzas, burgers, and steaks, part of side dishes or as a side dish on its own with some butter, herbs, and garlic.

**Magical Uses**

Include button mushrooms to help with indecisiveness or if you are struggling to choose. Also good for clarity, especially when consumed before using psychic abilities. Eat a dish with mushrooms before or during the casting of glamour or love spells, or before performing illusion magic to increase the quality and strength.

**Healing Qualities**

Adding button mushrooms may help against brain diseases that target memory and language. Slice and expose the mushroom to sunlight for fifteen minutes before eating to get a large dose of vitamin D.

**CREMINI** (Agaricus Bisporus)

**AKA** Portobello Mushroom or Portabella or Crimini or Common White Mushroom or White Button or Brown Mushroom or Baby Bella

Cremini mushrooms are the mature version of button mushrooms, their color is usually darker and their taste a little stronger. Use cremini mushrooms in pastas, roasts, soups, casseroles, risottos, omelets, quesadillas, quiche, tarts, bruschetta, and salads. They also make a really good gravy or sauce.

**Magical Uses**

Include Cremini mushrooms to help with indecisiveness or if you are struggling to choose. Also good for clarity when consumed before using psychic abilities; or eat a dish with mushrooms before or during the casting of glamour, love, or illusion magic to improve the quality of spell work.

**Healing Qualities**

Adding Cremini mushrooms may help against brain diseases that target memory and language. Slice and expose the mushroom to sunlight for fifteen minutes before eating to get a large dose of vitamin D.

**SHIITAKE** (Lentinula Edodes)

**AKA** Sawtooth Oak Mushroom or Black Forest Mushroom or Black Mushroom or Golden Oak Mushroom or Oakwood Mushroom or Brown Oak or Chinese Black

Shiitake is a great replacement for bacon in pasta dishes. Other great ways to use shiitake is in rice, pasta, vegetarian dishes, soups, stews, stocks, and broths.

**Magical Uses**

If you are struggling with self-esteem, or with who you are, shiitake can help let your uniqueness shine through. Shiitake can help you be joyful or express joyfulness, and attract joy to the dwelling you consume your dish in.

**Healing Qualities**

Shiitake mushrooms can help boost your immune system and production of white blood cells.

**OYSTER MUSHROOM** (Pleurotus Ostreatus)

**AKA** Oyster Fungus or Hiratake or Pearl Oyster Mushroom

Use oyster mushrooms in stews, soups, stir fries, sauces, or use them as a side dish. This mushroom goes particularly well with beef.

### Magical Uses

If you are going through a personal transformation, or dabbling in transformation or glamour magic, oyster mushrooms will help smooth the way and hasten the process. Oyster mushrooms can be used before, on their own or part of sex magic rituals, to increase potency and lust.

### Healing Qualities

Improve heart health and boost your immune system when you add oyster mushrooms to your diet.

### PORCINI (Boletus Edulis)

**AKA** Penny Bun or Porcino or Cep or Steinpilz

Porcini is great both fresh and dried. Use them is salads, risottos, and pasta dishes as they are renowned for their woodsy aroma and earthy meaty flavor.

### Magical Uses

Eat a dish with porcini before going on a graveyard walk, attempting a séance or death stalking to help make contact easier and strengthen your connection with the other side.

Add porcini regularly if you wish for the ability to sense trickery and lies, and for the sight to pierce through the veil created by a glamour spell.

### Healing Qualities

Porcini can aid in weight loss, reduce inflammation, and is reported to kill colon cancer cells.

### ENOKI (Flammulina Filiformis)

**AKA** Snow Puff or Enokitake or Futu or Winter Mushrooms

It is important to cook enoki before eating, so don't add this to salad unless it has been sautéed. Enoki goes well with bacon, beef, and broccoli dishes.

## Magical Uses

To increase a feeling of family and unity, add enoki to your dish. For the same reason, add it to the first dinner dish shared with a newly adopted child, or when two families have joined and are now living as one, also known as stepfamilies or stepsiblings.

## Healing Qualities

They have been known to help slow down cancer growth, regulate immune systems, protect heart health, and improve brain function.

## CHANTERELLE (Cantharellus Cibarius)

**AKA** Egg Mushroom or Golden Chanterelle or Yellow Chanterelle or Pfifferling

This delicacy has a fruity and peppery taste. It is also one of the most popular mushrooms to be picked in the wild. To get the most out of the chanterelle, it must be cooked in fats like butter or cream.

## Magical Uses

Those fearful of losing their ill gained fortunes should add this to their meals once a day.

## Healing Qualities

Chanterelle mushrooms are high in vitamin B and are great for bone health.

## MAITAKE (Grifola Frondosa)

**AKA** Hen-of-the-woods

This peppery mushroom can be added to any savory dish, including soups, stews, and pasta dishes.

## Magical Uses

Deepen your connection to the earth and even commune with nature spirits by adding maitake mushrooms to your meal before meditating outside, preferably sitting or lying directly on the grass or ground. Other than being a wonderful experience, if you do it often enough you will be able to draw directly from the earth's energy.

## Healing Qualities

Lower your risk of heart disease when you regularly eat maitake mushrooms.

# Edible flowers

### **Flower Power**

While edible flowers have many nutrients your body needs, their visual presence stimulates the production of happy chemicals in the brain. Positive feelings are always stronger than negative ones, and they stimulate your mana. The happier and more positive you are while performing kitchen magic, the stronger the magical outcome.

Remember that not all flowers are edible and could make you very ill if consumed. Below is a list of flowers that are not only safe to eat, but healthy too.

# Flowers

**CARNATIONS** (Dianthus Caryophyllus)
**AKA** Grenadine or Clove Pink
Carnation petals can be candied, pickled, used as decoration on cakes, and even used in a base for cocktails.

**Magical Uses**
A dish with red carnations should be shared with the partner you wish to increase the level of passion, love, and sensuality with, or eaten during or as part of love spells.

A dish with yellow carnation will help you heal from disappointment, rejection, and hurt feelings caused by contempt.

Increase the bond between mother and child when sharing a dish with pink carnations.

Purple carnation is for attracting or gaining elegance, as well as to heal a heart scorned by unrequited love.

To attract pure love into your life, add white carnation to your dish.

**Healing Qualities**
Carnations can be used to treat coughs and colds.

**CHRYSANTHEMUMS** (Chrysanthemum Indicum)
**AKA** Mums or Chrysanths
Ranging in color and taste from peppery to cauliflower, the petals must be blanched before using. They add amazing taste to salads and are the perfect flavor to add to vinegar.

**Magical Uses**
Try white chrysanthemums for metaphysical protection and to make yourself temporarily invisible from evil spirits.

Red chrysanthemums to increase or speed healing.

Purple chrysanthemums can help increase passion or power.

To attract romance, pink chrysanthemums petals work best.

Consuming a dish with yellow or orange chrysanthemum petals will allow you to absorb mana from the sun for one full day. This energy can be redirected into energy harnessing, or purely for the increase of physical energy that lasts for several days. Not to be used too often as it can cause headaches.

**Healing Qualities**

Chrysanthemums can help increase blood flow to the heart.

**CLOVER** (Trifolium)

**AKA** Trefoil

Clovers are sweet, similar to anise. Clover leaves are great for salads, teas, and in mint jelly.

**Magical Uses**

Red clover can help you understand, as well as deepen, the connection between both the humans and the animals you come into contact with.

White clovers can help in overcoming fear and in surviving change.

**Healing Qualities**

Clovers can help improve circulation.

**DANDELIONS** (Taraxacum Officinalis)

**AKA** Lion's-tooth or Cankerwort or Irish Daisy or Monk's-head or Priest's-crown or Puffball or Blowball or Milk-gowan or Witch-gowan or Yellow-gowan

Flowers are best picked young when they are still sweet and honey-like in taste. They are good raw and steamed and sprinkled over salad or rice dishes.

**Magical Uses**

Use to temporarily and exponentially increase psychic abilities. Do not use twenty-four hours before planned hypnosis or astral travel.

**Healing Qualities**

Dandelions can help improve and stimulate the immune system.

**GLADIOLUS** (Gladiolus)

**AKA** Sword Lily or Marsh Gladiolus

Once the antlers are removed, the gladiolus is ready to use. Vaguely tasting like lettuce, gladiolus works best in spreads and mousses, or in salsa and fruit salads.

**Magical Uses**

Cure infatuation with gladiolus, or use this flower to enhance clarity of memories. It is also helpful in memory recovery, especially when combined with hypnosis.

**Healing Qualities**

Gladiolus can help improve mood and energy levels.

**HIBISCUS** (Hibiscus rosa-sinensis)

**AKA** N/A

Hibiscus taste a bit like cranberries with an orange twist. The flowers can be dried to make tea, or they can simply be sprinkled over salads.

**Magical Uses**

Use hibiscus to attract love, lust, passion, and prophetic dreams. It can also be used to repel evil spirits, and the effects of the Evil Eye cast on you by blood relatives.

**Healing Qualities**

Hibiscus fights inflammation and supports liver health.

## HOLLYHOCK (Alcea Rosea)
**AKA** N/A

The leaves, roots, and blossoms of this beautiful plant are edible, but very bland in taste. They work well with rice, chicken, and mushroom dishes and pastries, such as Vol-au-vent.

### Magical Uses

Serve hollyhock dishes, such as vol-au-vents or similar, at and as part of rebirth ceremonies. Or serve at harvest (or other appropriate) celebrations, as a way to show gratitude and attract abundance for the following season.

### Healing Qualities

Tea made from hollyhock is good for breathing and digestive tract problems.

## HONEYSUCKLE (Lonicera Japonica)
**AKA** Japanese Honeysuckle or White Honeysuckle or Chinese Honeysuckle

The flowers are sweet and like their names suggests, honey in flavor. Honeysuckle can be made into a great pancake syrup or as a sweetener in herbal tea. Don't be afraid to experiment with honeysuckle in sweet chicken and pork dishes, or even desserts.

### Magical Uses

Can be served to a love interest, or taken before, or during or as part of, a love binding ceremony.

A drink or dish with honeysuckle can help with and increase psychic visions, including seeing ghosts and spirits.

Also good for those who wish to approach and communicate with the bees in their gardens. If you do not have confidence in your magic when creating the dish, the infusion won't work properly or possibly at all. If this happens, you might get stung. Not advised for beginners.

### Healing Qualities

**NOTE**: The berries are highly poisonous. Only the flowers are edible. Not to be confused with the other two species of honeysuckle.

Honeysuckle tea can help urinary disorders, headache, diabetes, and rheumatoid arthritis. It can also be used to counter certain poisons.

**IMPATIENS** (Impatiens Waller Ana)

**AKA** Busy Lizzie or Touch-me-not or Snapweed or Patience

The flowers are sweet and generally used in salads, or to decorate summer drinks and punch bowls because they float so nicely.

### Magical Uses

Even if the garnish is not eaten, the magic of impatiens will spread into the salad or drink it is decorating as long as you allow at least thirty minutes before serving.

Impatiens will help with encourage forgiveness, ease a restless spirit, or a mind consumed by stress or desperation.

### Healing Qualities

Impatiens has great anti-inflammatory properties.

**JOHNNY-JUMP-UPS** (Viola ricolour)

**AKA** Wild Pansy or Ladies' delight or Jump-up-and-kiss-me or Heartsease or Pansy or Love-in-idleness

The soft wintergreen flavor of Johnny-jump-ups works well in soups, salads, and desserts. They can be used to decorate a cake, or add to a cheese platter that has soft cheese in the mix.

### Magical Uses

Increase power, vitality, and energy by adding Johnny-jump-ups to your cooking.

If you do a lot of manifestation and glamour spells, eat a dish of Johnny-jump-ups beforehand for faster manifestation and stronger illusions.

**Healing Qualities**

Johnny-jump-ups can help relieve minor aches and pains.

**LILAC** (Syringa Vulgaris)

**AKA** Common Lilac

The lemony floral taste varies from plant to plant, and is entirely edible. Add to sugars, teas, syrups, or use in a variety of sweet treats, from cheesecake to petit fours. Lilac sugar and bottled syrups make for fragrant and delightful magical gifts.

**Magical Uses**

Extend the playfulness of new love or the honeymoon period by including lilac daily, for example, by adding lilac sugar to your daily tea or main meal.

Lilac can be infused into a meal to bring a sense of peace, fun, and to banish internal bad energy.

**Healing Qualities**

Use lilac to reduce stress and anxiety.

**MARIGOLDS** (Tagetes Tenuifolia)

**AKA** Poor Man's Saffron or Herb of the Sun

Marigolds taste a lot like saffron, but remember that only the petals are edible. Sprinkle the orange petals in soups, spreads, rice dishes, and scrambled eggs for flavor and a yellow hew. The petals also go well in pasta dishes, herb butter, and salads.

**Magical Uses**

Marigolds can increase joy, happiness, positivity, and luck.

**Healing Qualities**

Consuming marigolds can help with skin conditions including bruising and varicose veins.

**NASTURTIUMS** (Tropaeolum Majus)

**AKA** Indian Cress

Use the stem of this peppery flower the way you would chives; use as a garnish on potatoes, pasta, gratins, stir fry, garlic bread, and salads. The blossoms are sweet and spicy and can be stuffed with mousse or added to savory appetizers. Pickle the seed pods and you have a replacement for capers.

**Magical Uses**

Use pink nasturtiums if you need a little help overcoming obstacles in your life.

The orange nasturtium gives you a boost of vigor.

The red nasturtium gives a boost in vitality.

The creamy vanilla ones are interchangeable with any of the above three.

**Healing Qualities**

Nasturtium can help combat coughs, sore throats, and colds.

**PEONY** (Paeonia Lactiflora)

**AKA** Semi-double or Anemone Flower or Full-double or Bomb

Parboil the fallen petals and sweeten for a tea-time treat. Add the petals to water or salad. Or float in bowels of punch and lemonade.

**Magical Uses**

If used as a garnish in drinks, allow for at least thirty minutes before serving to allow the magic to seep into the drink. Ward off nightmares and demons, or call on protection during storms and tornadoes with peony.

**Healing Qualities**

Peony may help reduce pain and swelling. It can prevent bad cholesterol, promote liver health, lower the risk of heart disease, and increase immunity.

**PERENNIAL PHLOX** (Phlox Paniculata)

**AKA** Garden Phlox

This plant grows upright and comes in shades of red, purple, and pink. It is spicy in taste and works well in fruit salads.

**Magical Uses**

Share a meal that includes this flower to improve, or create, a bond of harmony, compatibility, and unity, in those participating.

Consume before meditating to ignite or grow your inner harmony, and find yourself getting along better with people.

**Healing Qualities**

**NOTE:** The *annual* phlox is not edible (The creeping version that grows near the ground).

The perennial phlox has been known to help treat stomach and intestinal problems, such as aches or indigestion.

**PINEAPPLE GUAVE** (Feijoa Sellowians)

**AKA** Feijoa or Guavasteen

You can use the leaves, fruit, and even the stem of this exotic tasting fruit can be used in a multitude of sweet dishes including smoothies, homemade ice-cream, sorbets, mousses, cheesecakes, and sponge cake.

**Magical Uses**

Pineapple guave can be used when you need a boost perseverance.

**Healing Qualities**

This plant has been known to improve the immune system, increase metabolism, lower cholesterol, aid in weight loss, improve digestion, and increase blood circulation.

## PRIMROSE (Cucurbita)

**AKA** Cowslip or Butter Rose or Early Rose or Easter Rose or Golden Rose or Lent Rose

As far as what this sweet but bland flower brings to the dish, the answer is color. You can try adding them to salads or vegetable dishes.

### Magical Uses

Eat a dish of primrose before working with beauty, youth, and glamour spells to enhance and lengthen the time of outcome.

### Healing Qualities

Primrose can help lessen premenstrual symptoms such as irritability, depression, back ache, and fatigued.

## QUEEN ANNE'S LACE (Daucus Carota)

**AKA** Wild Carrot and Bishop's Lace

Thank this flower for your modern day carrot, which is why it has a mild carrot flavor. Use the little white flowers in salads.

### Magical Uses

Queen Anne's lace will encourage psychic dreams. Best used by those experienced in lucid dreaming as the dreams can become intense but easily controlled by the experienced. The control will not alter the psychic dream, but controlling the dream will help it be delivered in a friendlier manner.

### Healing Qualities

**NOTE**: This flower is easily found in the wild; the problem is, so is Wild or Poison Hemlock. They are closely related and look almost the same, and even grow in the same areas. You are better off purchasing this one from a reputable supplier, but if you are insistent, the best way to distinguish the two is as follows: Queen Anne's Lace has a hairy stem. The stems of Wild Hemlock are smooth, hairless, and hollow with purple spots. Avoid Wild Hemlock at all cost.

Queen Anne's Lace works well as the main ingredient for a hangover remedy, or to help settle gastrointestinal issues.

**ROSE** (Rosa Rugosa)
**AKA** N/A

Taste very much depends on soil conditions the rose bush was grown in, as well as type and color. Rose petals can taste fruity or minty or spicy, but remember to cut off the white bit that was attached to the flower itself as this part is bitter. And the darker the rose, the more pronounced its flavor.

Use rose petals in homemade ice-creams, cold desserts, salads, or to flavor jellies, spreads, and punchbowls alike. You can also flavor butter that takes crackers, and toast, to the next level. Store a few bottles away as both make fantastic magical gifts that can be grabbed from the shelf. Add to homemade strawberry jam or bottle as a syrup, or teas.

**Magical Uses**

Eat a meal that has rose petals before bedtime to inspire prophetic dreams, especially those of future loves.

Eat before performing, or during and as part of, a love spell or ritual. While cooking and eating, concentrate on the qualities you want your future love to have, or focus on their face if you already have someone in mind.

Rose petals can also increase and heighten feminine intuition, and to help lessen the burden of grief, or uplift the spirit.

**Healing Qualities**

Rose petals act as an anti-inflammatory, can help lessen the symptoms of premenstrual stress and menopause, help an upset stomach, sore throats, and colds.

## SCENTED GERANIUMS (Pelargonium species)
**AKA** N/A

The variety and the taste go hand in hand when it comes to geraniums, i.e. the lemon-scented variety will have a lemony taste, and so on. So expect anything from citrus to spice to fruity to floral. Depending on what you have, it can be added to salad, or to flavor and decorate a cake. The rose one is most popular when used for cakes.

**Magical Uses**

Use geranium to relieve pain and hatred attached to old memories. It also helps to open a closed-off heart.

**Healing Qualities**

**NOTE**: The citronelle variety is not edible.

Geranium can be used to relieve anxiety and depression, as well as pain and infection.

## SUNFLOWER (Helianthus Annu)
**AKA** N/A

Use the shelled seeds in salads, breads, or granola bars. Unopened buds tastes similar to artichokes and can be steamed as such. Once the bittersweet flower opens, use the petals the same way you would chrysanthemums.

**Magical Uses**

Consume before performing healing work to improve the outcome and lessen personal mana expended during.

The petals can also be used to increase confidence and inner happiness.

> If you are an empath dealing closely with or with many people on a day to day basis, place the seeds (still shelled) in the activation bowl. Focus your intent, imagine each seed giving you an invisible shield that only you can sense. Leave in the

bowl for three days, repeating the focusing of intention every morning for three mornings. Keep on hand and nibble throughout the day to guard against the negative emotions of others. Depending on how much energy you harnessed and focused into it, you might even be able to sense the shield go up around you.

**Healing Qualities**

The petals have been used to help respiratory infections, while the seeds are known to help with coughs and colds.

**SWEET WOODRUFF** (Galium Odoratum)

**AKA** Wild Baby's Breath

Nutty with a hint of vanilla, this flower is best used in cakes, syrups, punch, or homemade lemonade.

**Magical Uses**

Woodruff can help sway victory in your favor and attract prosperity.

**Healing Qualities**

**NOTE**: When consumed in large amounts, Sweet woodruff can cause blood-thinning. Sweet woodruff can be used to relieve migraines and nerve pain.

**TUBEROUS BEGONIA** (Begonia x Tuberose)

**AKA** N/A

The leaves, flowers, and stems of the tuberous begonia are edible and have a citrus-sour taste. The petals can be used in salads or as a garnish, while the stems can be used if you don't have rhubarb on hand.

**Magical Uses**

Serve a dish with tuberous begonias to your family or a group that needs to increase its level of communication and understanding.

If you need to increase a sense of caution and consideration, whether in yourself or another, add tuberous begonia to the dish.

**Healing Qualities**

**NOTE**: Do not serve to individuals who suffer from regular bouts of gout, kidney stones, or rheumatism.

**VIOLETS** (Viola)

**AKA** Viola

Sweet and floral, add the small young leaves and flowers to salads, while the heart shaped leaves can be cooked and served like cabbage. Crystalize in sugar and use to decorate cakes, drinks, sorbets, and other desserts.

**Magical Uses**

Increase wisdom and humility with a violets.

**Healing Qualities**

Help combat strain, physical, and mental exhaustion with violets.

Cassandra Sage

# Miscellaneous

As with everything in life, there are always the few odd ones out. Here is a list of common kitchen ingredients along with their magical properties.

**BEEF** (N/A)
**AKA** N/A

Depending on the meat variety and cut, meat can be prepared in a variety of ways and paired with a variety of herbs, spices, vegetable, and some fruits.

**Magical Uses**

Beef can help lesson aggression. It encourages bliss, excitement, and prosperity. Also used to increase spiritual protection and increase your mana.

**Healing Qualities**

Rich in high-quality protein, vitamins, and minerals, beef also improves muscle growth and maintenance.

## BUCK/ DEER/RHEINDEER

**AKA** Game or Venison

From pies to pan fried, it all depends what cut you have on how you would cook it. The gamey wild taste and aroma varies from specie to specie, which will influence how you choose to prepare it. Goes well with root vegetables.

**Magical Uses**

Attract and encourage elegance, grace, and refinement, from within and outward.

It can be used to increase feminine magic, but beware that it will be wild and can cause emotions to run high (especially when cast as a coven). Effects only last a few hours.

**Healing Qualities**

Game is packed with a variety of vitamins, minerals, and protein.

## CHICKEN (N/A)

**AKA** N/A

Roasted, braised, grilled, fried, added to pie, poitjie, stew, or casserole, or even on the fire. Chicken is versatile and takes on flavor well. You can try for sweet with honey bastes, or stuff with lemon, butter, and rosemary for a citrus twist, or crumb, or simply salt. Your options are endless.

**Magical Uses**

Chicken has an even stronger effect when served and intended for a group, as opposed to just one person.

If your coven has performed any fertility, healing, or protection ceremonies, serve a chicken dish before, or in place of, grounding ceremonies.

Chicken dishes can be served to encourage emotional healing and wellbeing, as well as providing a temporary layer of protection against emotional attacks. Even if the attacks are created from your own memory or feelings.

**Healing Qualities**

Chicken releases a mild form of tryptophan, which is linked to higher levels of 'happy' chemical called serotonin.

The fat under the skin helps speed up recovery of colds and flu, lung infections like bronchitis and pneumonia. This is the reason chicken soup makes you feel better when you are sick.

Chicken helps reduce the chances of heart disease.

There have also been links between chicken consumption and the reduction of cancer cells.

**COFFEE BEANS** (Coffea Arabica)

**AKA** N/A

Technically this is a fruit, or at least coffee beans come from a fruit called the coffee cherry. If you do happen to get your hands on the fruit, you will find they are sweet and fragrant, and have the same magical properties.

Enjoyed by millions as a beverage, not everyone considers adding coffee beans to their cooking. Ground up coffee beans enhances the flavor of baked goods and desserts that include chocolate or cocoa, or it can be included in a spice rub for pork or beef.

**Magical Uses**

Coffee is commonly used before and during coven rituals to stimulate the mana in the room.

Coffee can neutralize negative energies being sent your way as well as being able to break mild curses.

Ward off depression and attract longevity, or include in longevity rituals to strengthen.

**Healing Qualities**

Good quality coffee (Beans) is brilliant for liver health, helps the body process sugar, and can help prevent Parkinson's. And it helps strengthen your DNA.

**COCOA BEANS** (Cucurbita)

**AKA** N/A

It is a seed, but not one commonly found in households. Most of us are more familiar and comfortable using cocoa or cacao powder. While cocoa powder and cacao powder come from the same tree pod, they are not the same end product.

Cacao is another term for when the beans have been put through a process that does not use heat, and is referred to a raw cacao. It is usually very light in color, and more bitter than cocoa.

Cocoa is the Dutch-processed. Heat is used to process it, so it is no longer considered raw. It tends to be cheaper and more readily available to use.

The two can be interchanged, but remember that cocoa powder in baked goods usually requires baking soda, and exchanging it for cacao might lead to needing more sugar to offset the bitterness.

Both seeds and powder are earthy, rich, and bitter in taste. Either can be used in hot drinks, baked goods, and desserts and to make home-made chocolate and chocolate treats.

Do make sure your cocoa or cacao powder is of high quality, and is part of the Fair Trade movement.

**Magical Uses**

Either powder can stir feelings of happiness, compassion, forgiveness, acceptance of self, as well as love for others and themselves. This is what makes this such a perfect ingredient in baked magical gifts.

**Healing Qualities**

Cocoa and cacao can enhance your cognitive responses, better your mood, and reduces your chance of heart disease.

Cacao is cram packed with nutrients and increases blood flow to the brain. While cocoa does still have some of this healing power, it is mostly diminished due to the heat process it goes through.

**CHAMOMILE TEA** (Matricaria Chamomilla)

**AKA** N/A

Chamomile has a sweet, almost fruity taste, with bitter undertones. Like other teas, you can add milk and sweeten to taste with honey.

**Magical Uses**

Chamomile can attract opportunities to make money.

Sufferers of nightmares, night terrors, and sleep paralysis can benefit from a cup of chamomile before bed. While drinking, think only sweet thoughts about what you want to dream about or about things that make you smile.

Drink four times a day if you are seeking or struggling with poise, humility, and grace. Or if you find your feminine magic is out of balance.

Good for those who are struggling with meditation or astral traveling, consume before attempting to perform either.

## Healing Qualities

Chamomile works as a mild sedative and can help stave off the effects of depression.

## EGGS (Ovum)
**AKA** N/A

There are a dozen ways to cook and eat eggs on their own, and dozens of dishes and baked goods that require them. Eggs act well as a binding agent and good for coating food before crumbing. You can even drink it raw when combined with the right ingredients.

### Magical Uses

**NOTE**: Do not reuse eggs used in Oomancy practices or rituals.

Eggs can help encourage prophetic dreams, or allow your vision to see any oncoming dark energies, spirits, or the glare of the Evil Eye, as well as the direction they are coming from.

### Healing Qualities

Eggs aid in eye and bone health, the immune system, metabolism, and liver function, as well as brain development in babies when consumed by the mother during pregnancy.

> *"Never throw away broken eggshells without crushing them first," my mother said as she crushed them with a pestle and mortar. "Else evil spirits, dark fae, and nasty sprites can use them to travel to other worlds, and bring back other dark entities, magicks, and strife to release upon our world."*

## FISH
**AKA** N/A

Bake, sauté, boil, grill, or even fried, most fish goes well with lemon, parsley, and tartar sauce.

### Magical Uses
Fish is used to encourage fertility, love, and lust.

To increase psychic powers and awareness, or if you are having trouble exploring your unconsciousness, try fish.

### Healing Qualities
While you shouldn't have it every day, fish aids in healthy brain function, and the development of vision and nerves in infant (during pregnancy). However, you should avoid raw fish (unless its tuna), as well as the following options during pregnancy:

- Bigeye tuna.
- King mackerel.
- Marlin.
- Orange roughy.
- Swordfish.
- Shark.
- Tilefish.

Fatty fish is good for a variety of other health reasons, including cholesterol and as a migraine buster and for lowering blood pressure.

## HONEY (N/A)
**AKA** N/A

The taste and golden color is very much dependent on the flowers the bees collected pollen from. Even in comb form, or partially crystalized, honey is sweet and pleasant to eat. Use honey for grilling, roasting, or to replace sugar in tea, porridge, or baked goods.

Do try and purchase locally produced and sourced honey.

Purchase high grade honey that has not been radiated or diluted. Labels differ from country to country. In some countries, the label must mention IF the product is radiated. In other countries, the labels must mention if the product is NOT radiated. So please do a little research when you add honey to your shopping list and before you place it in your basket.

**Magical Uses**

Sweeten someone's feelings towards you with a magical treat made with honey.

Honey can be used to help end arguments. Sweeten thoughts and words when a honey treat or dish is shared.

Honey can be used to solidify a relationship by way of magical gift, sharing a dish, or when consumed during a binding ritual.

For when you are feeling tongue-tied, and for those who wish to be glib or who stumble over words, add honey to your cooking and baking as often as you can. Alternatively, place your jar of honey in your activation bowl for five days and take a spoonful whenever you need. While it is in the bowl, make sure to once a day focus your attention on the honey, imagining that every time you speak, that words of silver and gold come out of your mouth.

**Healing Qualities**

Honey is natures anti-depressant and can help with colds, sore throats, and congestion.

## LAMB /MUTTON (N/A)
**AKA** N/A

Whether you are cooking a whole leg, making Shepard's pie or curry, remember to add seasoning, cook slowly, and allow to rest a few minutes before serving or slicing.

**Magical Uses**

Lamb attracts, and encourages from within, caring, kindness, sensitivity, inner strength, and warmth of love.

**Healing Qualities**

Lamb is high in iron and vitamin B, along with being packed with anti-inflammatory properties.

## LINDEN TEA (Tilia)

**AKA** N/A

Refreshing with a lemony zest, it tastes good both cold and warm. Add sliced lemon and honey to taste,

### Magical Uses

Drink during divination and card reading for more accurate results.

A cup before astral traveling works particularly well for beginners and those struggling to transition.

Drink while in the creation stage of tulpa development.

### Healing Qualities

**NOTE**: Do NOT drink if you are pregnant or have heart problems.

Linden tea is good for promote relaxation, fight inflammation, alleviate pain, or to soothe an irritated digestive tract.

## LIVER

**AKA** N/A

Liver has a strong gamey smell and is not for the inexperienced to cook. If you need to make use of this ingredient and feeling worried, try turning it into pâté that can be spread over crackers or toast.

### Magical Uses

Consume for courage and power.

### Healing Qualities

With high amounts of amounts of iron, riboflavin, vitamin B12, vitamin A, and copper, a meal with liver can help reduce the chances of malnutrition, making it a good option for someone ill, someone recovering from illness, or needs to regain weight due to illness, ailment, or operation.

## MAPLE SYRUP (N/A)
**AKA** N/A

Pancakes, waffles, bacon, ice-cream, or in baked goods, maple syrup adds an unbeatable and distinctive sweetness.

Do be sure that your maple syrup is of good quality and ethically sourced and has not been radiated or diluted. Labels differ from country to country. In some countries, the label must mention IF the product is radiated. In other countries, the labels must mention if the product is NOT radiated. So please do a little research before you add maple syrup to your shopping list.

### Magical Uses
Maple syrup will bring balance and stimulate an internal feeling of happiness.

### Healing Qualities
Maple syrup heals you on a cellular level, combating oxidative stress. Also, each spoonful is packed with nutrients.

## MILK AND CREAM (Cucurbita)
**AKA** N/A

This includes products made from milk or cream like yogurt, butter, ice-cream, chocolate, and cheese. An easy key ingredient for magical gifts.

For the best benefits, as in magic wise and on a cosmic karma level, try for locally sourced and unprocessed.

### Magical Uses
Milk and cream encourages good things to happen in our lives. Use as an ingredient to increase goodness, vitality, and health. Consume when you are looking for clarity on old memories, but

note that it will only help you remember the good memories, or the good parts of memories, better.

## Healing Qualities

Dairy is renowned for helping broken bones heal and improving bone health in general. This includes osteoporosis.

## PORK (N/A)
### AKA N/A

Depending on what cut of meat you have, will sway how you cook it. There is one rule: Never undercook pork, and be wary of adding salt as this is a very salty meat. It can be sweetened up with cherries, plums, prunes, apples, or honey.

## Magical Uses

If you feel life has become a little dull, why not stir up some chaos and create some dramatic energy? Use with caution, and not too often.

Pork can also be used to enhance, or take on similar magic properties as the other ingredients paired with it, usually with an exciting twist. By this account, a slice of pork roast, a pork chop, or even a single link of pork sausage, can be cooked with and imbued with the magic of several neighboring ingredients.

## Healing Qualities

Pork helps with blood cell formations, brain, and thyroid function.

## RABBIT/ HARE
### AKA N/A

You can flavor rabbit almost the same way you do chicken. This rich game meat works well as a slow roast or in a stew.

## Magical Uses

Call upon creativity, abundance, and success. Be warned that the effects are relatively fleeting, lasting only a day or two. If you are using it purely for creativity, there is a possibility you will feel lethargic and drained for several days after.

Rabbit can also give you the gift of foresight.

**Healing Qualities**

Rabbit is very heart-healthy and encourages the building and repairing of blood cells, muscle, and skin cells.

**ROOIBOS** (Aspalathus Linearis)

**AKA** N/A

Caffeine free and with a wonderful fragrance, rooibos is the perfect drink for ages six months and up. It can be served cool with honey, or warm with some milk and honey.

Like regular tea, this can be drunk in a multitude of ways, cold or warm.

**Magical Uses**

Drink rooibos tea to improve physical, mental, or spiritual health.

A cup of rooibos tea can ease grief caused from loss, no more than five cups a day.

**Healing Qualities**

Hydrating and perfect for those sensitive to caffeine. Rooibos tea also protects the brain from the effects caused by stress.

**SALT** (Sodium chloride)

**AKA** N/A

This refers to all the varieties: white, red, and sea salt. Salt has been used to flavor foods for centuries. It also helps meat retain moisture while cooking. We even use a little in some baked goods. And if you get creative with herb salts, you can easily bottle and use it as a magical gift.

**Magical Uses**

Salt cleanses, dispel, and protects your mana, from negativity and negative vibrations, allowing for positivity and more powerful magic.

**Healing Qualities**

Salt promotes hydration levels and helps the vascular system which transports nutrients, blood, and oxygen throughout the body.

**SEAWEED** (Algae)

**AKA** Sea Lettuce

There are several varieties of edible seaweed available, and all of them are salty. An obvious necessity for sushi, but it also makes for a great addition to salads.

**Magical Uses**

Very popular with practitioners that live along the coastal line; it can be consumed before making attempts to speak with sea spirits and ghosts of those who have died at sea or along the shore. You must be at least ankle deep in the ocean before attempting.

Consume before meditating near the water to draw on the oceans chaotic dark water energy. Especially during the three days of full moon at dusk and dawn, when water is charged with both sun and moon energy. This energy makes for good bouts of creativity, spell casting, tulpamancy, emotional healing, and mutual dreaming.

This meditation can also be a bonding experience for a coven of predominantly women, usually performed before a festival, celebration, or gatherings that include music and dancing.

**Healing Qualities**

Seaweed is beneficial when it comes to skin health because of its anti-aging and anti-inflammatory properties.

## SUGAR (N/A)
**AKA** N/A

We bake, cook, and add sugar to our tea. It comes in mainly white and brown.

**Magical Uses**

Sugar is used to attract and manifest. You can choose to be specific about what you attract into your life, or you can let the sugar be influenced by, and strengthen, its fellow ingredients.

**TIP:** If you like sugar in your hot beverage or sprinkled over your cereal or oatmeal, why not place an Alchemist Key on your sugar bowl? This makes for a very easy way to incorporate kitchen witchcraft into your daily routine. Remember to be mindful about what you want to attract or manifest when adding and consuming.

**Healing Qualities**

Sugar supplies energy to your brain and cells. As with everything in life, moderation is key when it comes to sugar. If you consume more energy than what you dispel, the side effects could include weight gain.

\*\*\*

## SHELLFISH (N/A)
**AKA** N/A

Pastas, soups, or stuffed, the options depend on what shellfish you are using. Most pair well with a tomato or lemon base.

Do not thaw at room temperature, rather leave it in the fridge overnight. Remember to rinse under cold water before cooking. Wash your hands thoroughly after handling raw seafood and DON'T overcook.

### Magical Uses
- Increase lust when you share a dish of shellfish with someone.
- Shellfish is brilliant for increasing psychic awareness.

### Healing Qualities
Shellfish aids in weight loss. It also promotes a healthy brain, heart, and immune system.

## TEA (Camelia Sinensis)
**AKA** N/A

Whether you prefer white tea, green tea, black tea, or oolong, you are drinking a cup of tea that originates for the same plant. The variations in flavor depend on the time spent in the fermentation process: Tea leaves are left to air, the longer they are left, the darker they become in color. Not unlike how sliced apple or avocado turns brown the longer it is exposed to air. As the leaves dry they change from white to green, to oolong, and to black. In powdered form, green tea is called matcha.

You can drink it warm, add honey or sugar, milk or cream, or drink it as is. When it comes summer drinks, sweeten with honey or sugar, or experiment with fruits, lemon, or mint.

### Magical Uses
When it comes to tea magic, it works better when you heat water over fire or a small flame. It does not have to be a wood or coal fire, a gas stove will do the trick. Not only are you adding fire to its opposite element, water, which will give balance, but it forces you to pay attention to the water while it is boiling and activate the magic within the water to its fullest potential.

Soothe the bitterness and strain of the day with a cup of tea.

It can be used in a grounding ritual for one or for a coven. Iced tea can be made beforehand and stored in the refrigerator, or make a pot of tea for everyone to share.

Tea on its own can be used as a sort of mini ritual. A mini ritual like this is especially great for natural empaths, and for those with over stimulated psychic abilities. Or drink a cup in a nice quiet spot as a form of meditation, where you can quiet your mind and just be.

**Healing Qualities**

Tea can help ward off cancer and heart disease. It also assists with improving metabolism and gut health.

**WATER** ($H_2O$)

**AKA** N/A

We leave the most valuable ingredient, both magically and health wise, till last.

We drink it. Besides being a main ingredient in many dishes, we cook with it in a multitude of different ways, from braising, boiling, steaming, poaching to simmering. And its taste changes for the obvious reasons, like where it is sourced and bottled, but it is also influenced by temperature. If you are not a fan of the taste, try adding some fresh fruit, cucumber, or lemon to ice water.

**Magical Uses**

Water keeps us alive. It promotes healing, energy, and a sense of wellbeing. Because we use water in so many ways during cooking and baking, this is the perfect extra to any magical dish. The magic of water will seep into the neighboring ingredients, e.g. Pasta and rice will absorb the magical properties of the water while cooking.

Yet there is so much more to it. There is much debate about the exact number, but the human body is around fifty percent water. Meaning around fifty percent of us is one of the four elements that have had magical and spiritual significance in history, across many cultures, and civilizations.

As an element, it is considered feminine energy. Water represents intelligence and wisdom, softness, flexibility, and a force not to be underestimated. It symbolizes the very transition between birth and death: Life. Scientists, Greek philosophers, and many religions believe that water was here before anything else, even the other elements; making us part of the oldest, darkest, and most powerful element in the universe. Meaning the magic flowing within you, stems from a river as old as time itself.

The above is in its own a very good magical reason to stay hydrated and to protect our dwindling water sources.

**Healing Qualities**

Water helps regulate body temperature, lubricates joints, weight loss, skin clarity, youthful appearance, and so much more.

The Encyclopedia of Kitchen Witchery • 251

# About the Author

Southern Hemisphere born, Cassandra Sage is a multi-generational Kitchen Witch. When she is not in the kitchen brewing up a magical meal, Cassandra dabbles in writing. She decided to combine these two passions, and the idea for *The Encyclopedia of Kitchen Witchery* came into being. If she can pull herself away from the kitchen long enough, she hopes to complete a future follow-up.

# Index

Abdominal pains, 95

Abundance, 48, 71, *110, 136, 164, 188,*

*224, 245*

Abuse, *159*

Acceptance, 57, *238*

Aches, *130, 226, 228*

Achiote. *See* Annatto seed

Achiotillo seed. *See* Annatto seed

Acid reflux, 88, *202*

Adapt, *202*

Adoption, *154, 218*

Adventure, 64, 79, *187*

Affluence, *140*

Aggression, 48, 50, *235*

Ajmod. *See* Celery Seeds

Albahaca. *See* Basil

Ale cost. *See* Costmary

Alfalfa, **103**

Alholva. *See* Fenugreek

Allergies, *125*

Alligator Pear. *See* Avocado

Alligator Pepper. *See* Grains of

Paradise

Alligator Strawberry. *See* Lychee

Allspice, 56, **104**

Almonds, 70, 85, 86, 87, 95, **208**

Alzheimer's, *122, 127, 174*

Amadumbe. *See* Yam

Ancestors, *168*

Anemia, *112, 191, 199*

Anemone Flower. *See* Peony

Anger, *138, 165*

Animal communication, *123*

Animal guide, *123*

Animal magic, *138*

Anise seed, 48, 81, 88, **104**

Aniseed. *See* Anise seed

Anix. *See* Anise seed

Annatto seed, **105**

Anniversaries, *190*

Anniversary, *193*

Anti-aging, *247*

Anti-bacterial, *162, 170*

Anti-fungal, *165*

Anti-inflammatory, *104, 108, 127,*
*146, 164, 165, 170, 199, 200, 202, 225,*
*230, 242, 247*

Antioxidants, *117, 118, 119, 123, 142,*
*148, 153, 162, 171, 182, 187, 198*

Anxiety, 57, 88, 115, 132, *134, 195, 198,*
*201, 226, 231*

Aphrodisiac, *119*

Appetite, loss, *116*

Apple, 63, 81, 87, 94, 95, **176**

Apple, gold, *177*

Apple, green, 59, 63, 73, 79, 80, *177*

Apple, pink, 60, 63, 79, *177*

Apple, red, 52, 53, 62, 73, 79, *177*

Appreciation, *103*

Apricot, 56, 60, 64, 72, 79, 81, **178**

Arguments, *241*

Aril. *See* Mace

Arrowroot, **105**

Arrowroot Flour. *See* Arrowroot

Arthritis, *109, 111, 118, 127, 141, 149,*
*153, 165, 225*

Artichoke, 86, **150**

Asafetida. *See* Assafoetida

Asafoetida, **106**

Ashwagandha, **107**

Aspar Grass. *See* Asparagus

Asparagus, **151**

Asper Grass. *See* Asparagus

Aspirations, *171*

Asthma, *178*

Astragalus root, **107**

Astral travel, 57, 82, *117, 132, 145,*
*223, 238, 242*

Atsuete seed. *See* Annatto

Attention, *109, 188, 190*

Attract, *247*

Attraction, 52, *134*

Aubergine. *See* Eggplant

Aura, 59, 63, 81, 83, *124, 181*

Aura, 71

Avo. *See* Avocado

Avocado, 86, **179**

B Hirta. *See* White mustard

Baby Bella. *See* Cremini

Baby blues, *142*

Baby shower, *170*

Bacteria, 87, *127, 172, 188*

The Encyclopedia of Kitchen Witchery • 255

Bacterial, 134

Bailan Melons. *See* Honeydew

Balance, 82, *243*

Banana, 95, 98, **180**

Banishing, *111*, *143*, *146*, *147*, *172*

Baobab, **179**

Baptism, *185*

Barbary Fig. *See* Prickly Pear

Basil, 49, 56, 70, 71, 72, 81, 82, 83, 88,
89, **108**

Basilic. *See* Basil

Basilici Herba. *See* Basil

Bay Laurel. *See* Bay Leaf

Bay leaf, 56, 86, 88, **108**

Bearberry. *See* Cranberry

Beauty, 61, 63, 79, 82, *109*, *133*, *145*,
*166*, *186*, *191*, *192*, *201*, *205*, *229*

Bee balm. *See* Lemon Balm

Beef, 48, 50, 56, **234**

Bees, *224*

Beet. *See* Beetroot

Beet Powder. *See* Beetroot

Beetroot, **152**

Beetroot powder, **109**

Bell Peppers, **152**

Bengal Gram. *See* Chickpeas

Benne. *See* Sesame

Bergamot, **110**

Better times, 48, *199*

Bible Leaf. *See* Costmary

Bija. *See* Annatto seed

Binding, *241*

Bird's Foot. *See* Fenugreek

Birth defects, preventative, *161*

Birthday, *190*

Bishop's Lace. *See* Queen Anne's
Lace

Bitterness, *248*

Black Caraway. *See* Black Cumin

Black Cumin, **111**

Black Elder. *See* Elderberry

Black Forest Mushroom. *See*
Shitake

Black Mushroom. *See* Shitake

Black mustard, 83, **111**

Black pepper, 58, 79, 82, 83, 87, **112**

Black Seed. *See* Black Cumin

Black tea, 63, 73, 90, *See* Tea

Blackberry, 73, 94, **180**

**Blackberry Leaf**, 112

Black-eyed Peas, **153**

Bladder infections, *165*

Blessings, *185*

Bliss, 48, 50, 56, *235*

Bloating, 95, *116*

Blood cell formation, *244*

Blood cells, *245*

Blood circulation, *106, 140, 229*

Blood clotting, *141, 184*

Blood flow, 86, *222, 238*

Blood pressure, *109, 111, 118, 119,
120, 123, 127, 128, 130, 132, 133, 140,
151, 152, 154, 156, 159, 164, 168, 169,
171, 181, 188, 190, 191, 197, 201, 203,
204, 208, 210, 211, 240*

Blood sugar, *109, 111, 112, 113, 114,
126, 130, 137, 141, 149, 156, 173, 180,
188, 190, 208, 210, 211, 237*

Blood Turnip. *See* Beetroot

Blowball. *See* Dandelions

Blue Daisy. *See* Chicory

Blue Dandelion. *See* Chicory

Blue Sailor. *See* Chicory

Blueberry, 59, 63, 71, 73, 79, 81, 83, 92,

Bockshornklee. *See* Fenugreek

Bockshornsame. *See* Fenugreek

Boerbone. *See* Fava beans

Bomb. *See* Peony

Bond, 83

Bone health, *138, 139, 159, 181, 183,
184, 185, 186, 188, 190, 191, 192, 201,
203, 209, 218, 239, 244*

Brain, *238*

Brain development, *239*

Brain disease, *215, 216*

Brain function, *112, 141, 172, 209,
218, 240, 244*

Brain health, 92, *154, 156, 173, 178,
181, 185, 187, 204, 209, 212, 248*

Brassica Alba. *See* White Mustard

Brazil Nut, **208**

Breathing problems, *224*

Bride, *186*

Brinjal. *See* Eggplant

Brinjal Eggplant. *See* Eggplant

Broad Bean. *See* Fava beans

Broccoli, 90, 93, 96, **153**

Broken bones, *244*

Bronchitis, *105, 236*

# The Encyclopedia of Kitchen Witchery • 257

Brown Mushroom. *See* Cremini

Brown Mustard, **113**

Brown Oak. *See* Shitake

Bruising, *227*

Buck, **235**

Bulb Onion. *See* Onion

Bullying, *159*

Burnet, **113**

Burnet-bloodwort. *See* Burnet

Busy Lizzie. *See* Impatiens

Busy mind, 56, *183*

Butter Rose. *See* Primrose

Butterbean, 56, **151**

Button Mushroom, 58, **215**

Cabbage, 88, **154**

Cacao, 48, *See* Cocoa Beans

Cactus Pear. *See* Prickly Pear

Caffeine overdose, *121*

Calcium, *155*

Calm, 49, 53, 70, *164*, *193*

Calmn, *184*

Canary Beans, **155**

Cancer, 89, *115*, *124*, *127*, *128*, *137*, *138*, *140*, *145*, *149*, *153*, *154*, *156*, *158*, *163*, *164*, *170*, *171*, *172*, *174*, *181*, *183*, *187*, *191*, *196*, *197*, *199*, *201*, *203*, *212*, *217*, *218*, *236*, *249*

Cankerwort. *See* Dandelions

Cannabis, 61, 70, 90, **114**

Cantaloupe, 63, 72, **181**

Capalaga. *See* Cardamon

Capsicum. *See* Bell Peppers

Carberry. *See* Gooseberry

Cardamom. *See* Cardamon

Cardamon, 51, 81, 97, **116**

Cardiovascular, *201*

Cardiovascular disease, *153*, *201*

Caring, *241*

Carnations, **221**

Carrot, 50, 53, 59, 62, 93, **155**

Carroway Seeds, **115**

Cashew, 94, **209**

Casting, *134*, *160*, *161*, *165*

Catmint. *See* Catnip

Catnip, 73, 83, **117**

Catwort. *See* Catnip

Cauliflower, 90, **158**

Caution, *233*

Cayenne Pepper, 57, **117**

Celebrations, *160*

Celeriac Root. *See* Celery

Celery, 62, 83, 88, **158**

Celery Seeds, **118**

Cell damage. *See Oxidative stress*

Cep. *See* Porcini mushroom

Ceylon Cardamom. *See* Cardamon

Ceylon Cinnamon, **119**

Chakra, *124, 130*

Chakra activation, 70, *115*

Chamomile, 63, 73, 97, **238**

Champignon. *See* Button
   Mushroom

Chandrika. *See* Fenugreek

Change, *222*

Chanterelle, **218**

Chaos, 56, *244*

Chard. *See* Beetroot

Charm, *190*

Charm, feminine, 81, *186*

Cheer, 71

Cheerfulness, 55, 59, 81, *193*

Cherry, 53, 55, 57, 60, 64, 79, 81, **182**

Chervil, **120**

Chestnut, **209**

Chia seeds, 96, **119**

Chicken, 50, 58, 91, 96, 97, **235**

Chickpeas, **159**

Chicory, **120**

Childbirth, *185*

Chile Pepper. *See* Cayenne Pepper

Chili. *See* Chili pepper, *See* Chili
   pepper

Chili pepper, 53, 70, **121**

Chinese Black. *See* Shitake

Chinese Gooseberry. *See* Kiwi

Chinese Honeysuckle. *See*
   Honeysuckle

Chinese Mustard. *See* Brown
   Mustard

Chinese Parsley. *See* Cilantro

Chinese Star Anise. *See* Star Anise

Chives, 81, **121**

Choice, *183, 215, 216*

Cholesterol, 86, *104, 106, 109, 112,*
   *126, 127, 130, 137, 141, 148, 151, 164,*
   *166, 169, 171, 178, 179, 188, 202, 203,*
   *208, 210, 211, 228, 229, 240*

Chronic worry, 57

Chrysanthemum Weed. *See*
   Mugwort

The Encyclopedia of Kitchen Witchery • 259

Chrysanthemums, **221**

Chrysanths. *See* Chrysanthemum

Cilantro, 56, 82, 83, **122**

Cinnamon, 48, 51, 52, 57, 60, 62, 70, 81, *See* Ceylon Cinnamon

Circulation, *162*, *222*

Cives. *See* Chives

Clarity, 58, *131*, *215*

Cleansing, 58, 70, 81, 82, 83, *127*, *128*, *138*, *172*, *185*, *204*, *246*

Clementine. *See* Mandarin Oranges

Clove Pink. *See* Carnations

Clover, **222**

Cloves, 48, 51, 62, 91, **123**

Cobnut. *See* Hazel

Cocoa, 48, 53, 57, 94, *See* Cocoa Beans

Cocoa Beans, **237**

Coconut, 70, 71, **183**

Coffee Beans, 73, **236**

Coffeeweed. *See* Chicory

Cognitive function, *139*, *209*, *238*

Cold Hardy Mandarin. *See* Naartjie

Colds, *78*, *96*, *110*, *111*, *117*, *124*, *131*, *221*, *227*, *230*, *232*, *236*, *241*

Cole Florye. *See* Cauliflower

Colic, *117*, *131*

Collagen, *197*

Colon, *164*, *169*, *217*

Common Basil. *See* Basil

Common Garden Sage. *See* Sage

Common Kidney Bean. *See* Red Kidney Bean

Common Lilac. *See* Lilac

Common Mint. *See* Spearmint

Common Mushroom. *See* Button Mushroom

Common Onion. *See* Onion

Common Sorrel. *See* Sorrel

Common White Mushroom. *See* Cremini

Communication, 55, *158*, *170*, *232*

Communication, spirit, *195*

Compass Plant. *See* Rosemary

Compass Weed. *See* Rosemary

Compassion, 48, 53, 57, *238*

Compatibility, *228*

Conceive, *197*

Confidence, *159, 171, 187, 231*

Confusion, 56, *109*

Congestion, *241*

Connect to Nature, 56

Connection, *222*

Consecration, *138*

Consideration, *233*

Constipation, 88, 95, *201*

Contempt, *221*

Copper, *242*

Coriander. *See* Cilantro

Corn, **159**

Costmary, 62, **124**

Coughs, *105, 124, 131, 138, 144, 221,*
*227, 232*

Courage, 56, 58, 79, 82, *112, 113, 126,*
*242*

Courting, *193*

Coven, *55,* 82, *135, 160, 169, 194, 200,*
*236, 237, 246, 248*

Cowslip. *See* Primrose

Cramping, *116*

Cranberry, 71, 81, 89, 92, **182**

Cream, 53, 55, 57, **243**

Cream of Tartar Fruit. *See* Baobab

Creativity, 47, 53, 59, 70, 72, *131, 155,*
*189, 196, 245, 246*

Cremini, **215**

Crimini. *See* Cremini

Cronewort. *See* Mugwort

Cucumber, 53, **184**

Culinary Sage. *See* Sage

Cumin, 51, 52, **124**

Cummin. *See* Cumin

Cumquats. *See* Kumquat

Curcumin. *See* Tumeric

Cure-all. *See* Lemon Balm

Curry Leaves, **125**

Curse, bloodline, *162*

Curses, 57, 58, *112, 125, 162, 204, 237*

Cystitis, *112*

Dabberry. *See* Gooseberry

Dabino. *See* Date Fruit

Dandelions, 61, **222**

Date Fruit, **184**

Dates, 94, 95

Dayberry. *See* Gooseberry

Death, *131, 138, 139*

Death stalking, *117, 128, 153, 180,*
*217*

Deer, **235**

Defensive magic, *191*

Dementia, *127, 144*

Demons, *227*

Demotivated, *120*

Depression, 57, 70, 88, *110, 113, 142,*
*143, 174, 195, 231, 237, 239*

Desire, 51, 81, *116, 124, 134, 192*

Desperation, *225*

Determination, 56, 79, 104

Devil's Dung. *See* Assafoetida

Dewberry. *See* Gooseberry

Dhania. *See* Cilantro

Diabetes, *105, 124, 164, 171, 174, 181,*
*196, 199, 202, 203, 209, 225*

Diarrhea, 88, 95, *105, 110, 112, 135*

Digestion, *108, 110, 111, 115, 116, 117,*
*128, 130, 131, 135, 159, 163, 190, 191,*
*194, 197, 202, 209, 229*

Digestive problems, *174*

Digestive tract, *224, 242*

Dill, 82, 83, **125**

Dill Weed. *See* Dill

Disappointment, *221*

Diuretic, *138*

Divination, 81, *109, 122, 128, 138, 192,*
*242*

DNA, *237*

Double Bean. *See* Butterbean

Dragon's Mugwort. *See* Tarragon

Drama, *244*

Dream walk, *138*

Dream walking, 57

Dreaming, mutual, *117*

Dreaming, prophetic, *135*

Dreams, 70

Dreams, good, 64

Dreams, lucid, *117, 145*

Dreams, remembering, *117*

Dreams, sweet, 73, *145*

Dropsy Plant. *See* Lemon Balm

Dulce. *See* Celery

Dysentery, *112, 124*

Early Rose. *See* Primrose

Earth, magic, *123*

Easter Rose. *See* Primrose

Egg Mushroom. *See* Chanterelle

Eggplant, **160**

Eggs, 94, **239**

Egyptian Pea. *See* Chickpeas

Elderberry, 61, 73, 89, **185**

Electrolytes, *182*

Elegance, *221, 235*

Elephants Foot. *See, See* Yam

Elon herb. *See* Mugwort

Emotional attacks, 50

Emotional balance, *107*

Emotional connection, 55, 59

Emotional healing, *236, 246*

Empath, 55, 57, *120, 128, 136, 231, 249*

Empathy, *210*

Employment, *164, 197, 212*

Encensier. *See* Rosemary

Endurance, *202*

Endurance, mental, *120*

Enemies, *105, 139, 159*

Energies, dark, *239*

Energy, *148, 155, 171, 174*

Energy harnessing, *171, 205, 207,*
*222*

Energy healing, *115*

Energy, dramatic, *244*

Energy, feminine, *146*

Energy, masculine, *145*

Energy, negative, 57, 58, 70, 81, 83,
*105, 106, 112, 121, 122, 125, 129, 146,*
*204, 226,* 237

Energy, physical, 57, *225, 247*

Energy, water, *246*

English Lavender. *See* Lavender

English Thyme. *See* Thyme

Enoki, 91, 94, **217**

Enokitake. *See* Enoki

Epilepsy, *115*

Estragon. *See* Tarragon

Estrogen deficiency, *141*

European Black Elderberry. *See*
Elderberry

European Elderberry. *See*
Elderberry

European Sugar Beet. *See*
Beetroot

Evil Eye, 57, *105, 111, 125, 187, 223,*
*239*

Excitement, 50, *235*

Exhaustion, mental, *233*

Exorcism, *163*

The Encyclopedia of Kitchen Witchery • 263

Eye health, *137, 152, 154, 155, 160, 168, 172, 173, 179, 188, 193, 194, 195, 239*, 240

Faba Bean. *See* Fava Beans

Fabes. *See* Gooseberry

Fae, *210*

Fake scallion. *See* Leek

False Tangerine. *See* Naartijie

Fame, *177*

Family, *151, 169, 177, 218*

Fapes. *See* Gooseberry

Fatigue, 88

Fava Beans, **160**

Fayberry. *See* Gooseberry

Feaberry. *See* Gooseberry

Feabs. *See* Gooseberry

Feaps. *See* Gooseberry

Fear, 49, 56, 81, 82, *109, 158, 222*

Fearlessness, 81

Feelings, *170*

Feijoa. *See* Pineapple Guave

Feminine charm, 81, *145, 186*

Feminine energy, *146, 194, 250*

Feminine intuition, *230*

Feminine magic, 81, *145, 163, 186, 235, 238*

Fennel, 83, **126**

Fennel Flower. *See* Black Cumin

Fenogreco. *See* Fenugreek

Fenugreek, **126**

Fertility, 51, 81, *162, 168, 180, 184, 186, 188, 189, 197, 201, 236, 240*

Festival, *246*

Fever, *105, 110, 133, 146, 180*

Fiber, *120, 148, 153, 155, 180, 187*

Fidelity, 72, *116, 173, 198*

Field Balm. *See* Catnip

Fig, 81, **186**

Filbert. *See* Hazel

Filé, **127**

Finnochio. *See* fennel

Fish, 51, 54, 85, 87, 94, 95, **240**

Florence Fenne. *See* Fennel

Florentine Fennel. *See* Fennel

Flu, 96, *110, 117, 191, 236*

Fluid retention, *105*

Foenugreek. *See* Fenugreek

Forbidden Fruit. *See* Grapefruit

Forgiveness, 60, *238*

Fortune, *141*

Fortune Telling, *122*, *125*

Fortunes, ill gained, *218*

French Artichoke. *See* Artichoke

French Beans. *See* Green beans

French Parsley. *See* Chervil

French Thyme. *See* Thyme

Fresh Lemongrass. *See*

   Lemongrass

Friends, *169*

Friendship, 55, 57, 59, 60, 81, 82, *114*,

   *135*, *151*, *159*, *177*, *182*, *193*, *194*

Full-double. *See* Peony

Fun, 57, *115*, *118*, *137*, *152*, *226*

Funerals, *131*

Futu. *See* Enoki

Future, *177*

Future, bright, 80

Game. *See* Buck

Garbanzo Bean. *See* Chickpeas

Garden Basil. *See* Basil

Garden Burnet. *See* Burnet

Garden mint. *See* Spearmint

Garden Parsley. *See* Parsley

Garden peas. *See* Peas

Garden Phlox. *See* Perennial Phlox

Garden Sage. *See* Sage

Garden Sorrel. *See* Sorrel

Garden Strawberry. *See*

   Strawberry

Garden Thyme. *See* Thyme

Gardeners, *122*

Garlic, 81, 82, 83, 91, 96, **127**

Gas, 95, *108*, *110*, *116*, *126*, *131*, *148*

Gastrointestinal issues, *230*

Ghosts, 57, 61, *162*, *224*

Ghosts, sea, *246*

GI, *105*

Ginger, 55, 70, 79, 81, 86, 92, 96, 97,

   **128**

Gladiolus, **223**

Glamour, 53, *145*, *179*, *184*, *187*, *205*,

   *215*, *216*, *217*, *226*, *229*

Glib, *241*

Globe Artichoke. *See* Artichoke

Gloom, *110*

Goals, *185*

Goat Pea. *See* Black-eyed peas

Goggle Berry. *See* Gooseberry

The Encyclopedia of Kitchen Witchery • 265

Golden Chanterelle. *See* Chanterelle

Golden Oak Mushroom. *See* Shitake

Golden Rose. *See* Primrose

Goober. *See* Peanut

Good fortune, 49, 81, *106, 136, 162*

Good health, *171*

Good things, 50, 53, 83, *243*

Goodness, 50, 55, 57, 63, *243*

Goodwill, 58, 82, *136*

Gooseberry, 64, 79, 92, 94, **186**

Goosegob. *See* Gooseberry

Goosegog. *See* Gooseberry

Gout, *120, 127*

Grace, *186, 235, 238*

Grains of Paradise, **128**

Grapefruit, 64, **187**

Grapes, **188**

Grapes, green, *188*

Grapes, purple, 64, *188*

Grapes, red, 53, 61, 64, *188*

Gratitude, 72, *182, 195, 224*

Graveyard walk, *217*

Graveyard walking, 55, 61, 79, 81, *117, 125, 127*

Greek Clover. *See* Fenugreek

Greek Hay. *See* Fenugreek

Green Artichoke. *See* Artichoke

Green beans, **161**

Green Cardamom. *See* Cardamon

Green Onion. *See* Scallion

Green peas. *See* Peas

Green tea, 73, 90, *See* tea

Grenadine. *See* Carnations

Grief, *141, 230, 245*

Grizzle berry. *See* Gooseberry

Groser. *See* Gooseberry

Groset. *See* Gooseberry

Ground Nut. *See* Peanut

Grounding, 49, 56, 58, 71, *126, 165, 248*

Grounding ceremonies, *236*

Growth, *193*

Guava, **188**

Guavasteen. *See* Pineapple Guave

Guinea Grains. *See* Grains of Paradise

Guinea Pepper. *See* Grains of
  Paradise

Gumbo Filé. *See* Filé

Gut health, *120, 125, 127, 137, 164,*
  *165, 171, 172, 178, 180, 185, 199, 208,*
  *249*

Halloween, 79

Handfastings, *185*

Hangover, *202, 230*

Hangover, preventative, *196*

Happiness, 48, 53, 56, 60, 63, 64, 71,
  72, 79, 81, *105, 110, 127, 132, 155,*
  *170, 182, 186, 192, 198, 202, 226, 231,*
  *238, 243*

Hare, **244**

Haricots Verts. *See* Green beans

Harmony, *228*

Harvard Beet. *See* Beetroot

Harvest festival, *160, 190, 224*

Haunting, *162*

Hazel, **210**

Hazelnut. *See* Hazel

Headaches, *225*

Healing, 73, *179, 192, 221, 231, 249*

Healing magic, *138*

Healing, emotional, 104

Healing, spirit, *128*

Healing, spiritual, *165*

Health, *198,* 243

Health, spiritual, *245*

Healthy skin, *113*

Heart, *106, 125, 126, 128, 156, 161, 167,*
  *192, 217, 218, 219, 221, 231, 249*

Heart attack, 86

Heart broken, *131, 151, 202*

Heart disease, 95, *109, 119, 124, 130,*
  *145, 149, 152, 160, 163, 169, 171, 179,*
  *191, 196, 201, 203, 209, 228, 236, 238*

Heart function, *203*

Heart health, *136, 154, 173, 180, 181,*
  *182, 185, 187, 188, 189, 190, 191, 194,*
  *195, 197, 198, 207, 209, 245, 248*

Heart, balance, *107*

Heart, broken, *126*

Heartburn, *116, 126*

Heartsease. *See* Johnny-jump-ups

Hemorrhoids, *112*

Hemp, 61, 70, 90, **129**

Hen-of-the-woods. *See* Maitake

Herb of the Sun. *See* Marigolds

The Encyclopedia of Kitchen Witchery • 267

Herbe Aux Couronnes. *See* Rosemary

Herbe de Joseph. *See* Hyssop

Herbe Sacrée. *See* Hyssop

Herbe Sainte. *See* Hyssop

Hibiscus, 73, 97, **223**

Hing spice. *See* Asafoetida

Hiope. *See* Hyssop

Hiratake. *See* Oyster Mushroom

Hisopo. *See* Hyssop

Hoarhound. *See* Horehound

Hollyhock, **224**

Holy Basil, **130**

Honey, 97, **240**

Honey Plant. *See* Lemon Balm

Honey-blob. *See* Gooseberry

Honeydew, 53, **189**

Honeymoon, *226*

Honeysuckle, 61, **224**

Hope, 81, 82, *136, 141, 202*

Horehound, **130**

Hormones, *107*

Horseradish, 81, **161**

Hot Basil. *See* HOLY BASIL

Hot Peppers. *See* Chili pepper, *See* Chili pepper

Housewarming, *170*

Hren. *See* Horseradish

Hu Lu Ba. *See* Fenugreek

Huang Qi. *See* Astragalus

Humility, *233, 238*

Hydration, *171, 182, 184, 195, 246*

Hyper activity, *109*

Hypnosis, 52, *145, 223*

Hyssop, **131**

Identity, *199*

Ilachi. *See* Cardamon

Illness, *127, 243*

Illusion, *215, 216*

Illusion magic, *187*

Immune, 248

Immune system, *104, 124, 125, 127, 140, 166, 168, 171, 172, 185, 188, 190, 193, 194, 195, 209, 216, 217, 218, 223, 228, 229, 239*

Impatiens, **225**

Indecisiveness, *131, 215, 216*

India Winter Cherry. *See* Ashwagandha

Indian Cress. *See* Nasturtiums

Indian fig. *See* Prickly Pear

Indian Ginseng. *See* Ashwagandha

Indian Mustard. *See* Brown
Mustard

Indigestion, *131, 143, 158, 228*

Infections, 113, *130, 134, 231,* 232, 236

Infidelity, 83, *116, 155, 203*

Inflammation, 87, 95, *109, 114, 129,*
*143, 153, 155, 159, 163, 173, 180, 183,*
*185, 192, 197, 205, 209, 210, 217, 223,*
*242*

Inflammation, chronic, 88

Inhibitions, *71, 192*

Inhibitions, lessen, 79

Initiations, *185*

Inner demons, *112*

Inner self, *144*

Inner truth, *207*

Insight, *106, 160*

Insomnia, 88, 132

Inspiration, *108, 131*

Intentions, hide, *105*

Intestinal problems, *228*

Intimacy, *173*

Invocation ritual, *187*

Irish Daisy. *See* Dandelions

Iron, *111, 155, 242*

Irritability, 47, *104*

Irritable stomach, *104*

Jamaican Pepper. *See* Allspice

Japanese Honeysuckle. *See*
Honeysuckle

Japanese Horseradish. *See* Wasabi

Jaundice, *134*

Jealousy, 83, *112, 192*

Job, new, *197*

Johnny-jump-ups, **225**

Joint pain, *111, 123, 147*

Joints, *250*

Journey, *180*

Joy, 58, *142, 216, 226*

Jufa. *See* Hyssop

Jump-up-and-kiss-me. *See*
Johnny-jump-ups

Kalonji. *See* Black Cumin

Khren. *See* Horseradish

Kidney beans, 52, 86, *See* Red
Kidney Beans

Kidney stones, *142, 191*

The Encyclopedia of Kitchen Witchery • 269

Kidneys, *121*

Kindness, 59, 63, 71, 79, 80, 81, *203,*
*241*

Kiss, 54

Kiwi, 61, 71, 72, 79, 98, **190**

Knowledge, *63*, 71, *197, 209*

Krishna Tulsi. *See* Basil

Kumquat, 97, **190**

Lactating, *126*

Ladies' delight. *See* Johnny-jump-
ups

Lamb, 88, **241**

Lamb Mint. *See* Spearmint

Lavender, 73, 81, 82, **132**

Laziness, *120*

Leaf Mustard. *See* Brown Mustard

Leek, 88, 96, **163**

Lemon, 51, 59, 63, 70, 71, 72, 82, 91, 92,
96, **191**

Lemon Balm, 56, **132**

Lemon Beebrush. *See* LEMON
VERBENA

Lemon Verbena, **133**

Lemongrass, 96, **132**

Lent Rose. *See* Primrose

Lentils, 96, **163**

Lethargy, 57, *174*

Lettuce, **164**

Libido, *140*

Lichi. *See* Lychee

Licorice, **133**

Lies, *217*

Lilac, **226**

Lima Bean. *See* Butter beans

Lime, 71, 79, **192**

Linden tea, **242**

Lion's-tooth. *See* Dandelions

Liquorice. *See Licorice*

Litchi. *See* Lychee

Little Dragon. *See* Tarragon

Liver, *239*, **242**

Liver health, *151, 152, 223, 228, 237*

Loneliness, 48, 51, 62, *124*

Longevity, 59, 60, 63, 70, 71, 72, 81,
*107, 152, 179, 180, 191, 196, 198, 237*

Loss, *139, 152, 245*

Lovage, 83, **134**

Love, 48, 51, 52, 53, 54, 57, 59, 60, 62,
63, 70, 71, 72, 73, 79, 80, 81, *109, 111,*
116, 117, *136, 139, 142, 143, 151, 152,*

*155, 158, 159, 165, 166, 169, 172, 177, 179, 182, 188, 189, 190, 191, 193, 196, 197, 198, 199, 201, 202, 203, 204, 208, 209, 211, 215, 216, 221, 223, 224, 226, 230, 238, 240, 241*

Love Apple. *See* Tomato

Love Fruit. *See* Mango

Love, platonic, *114*

Love, unrequited, *221*

Love-in-idleness. *See* Johnny-jump-ups

Love-in-mist.. *See* Black Cumin

Lucerne. *See* alfalfa

Lucid dreaming, *229*

Luck, 49, 53, 55, 60, 63, 64, 71, 79, 81, *104, 122, 123, 128, 141, 143, 154, 162, 200, 201, 203, 226*

Lung Health, *198*

Lust, 51, 53, 61, 64, 73, 83, *134, 155, 179, 184, 188, 192, 197, 199, 209, 211, 217, 223, 240, 248*

Lustful, *201*

Lustful eye, *201*

Lychee, 61, 71, **192**

Maangelwurzel Mangel. *See* Beetroot

Mace, **134**

Mace Blades. *See* Mace

Mackerel Mint. *See* Spearmint

Madagascar Bean. *See* butterbean

Maggie Plant. *See* Lovage

Magic abilities, latent, *116*

Magic, feminine, *145, 163, 186*

Magic, illusion, *187*

Magic, similarity, *167*

Magic, strengthen, *104*

Magic, sympathetic, *167*

Magical awareness, *194*

Magical connection, 55

Magnesium, *117*

Magnetism, 81, *119*

Maitake, 58, **218**

Maize. *See* Corn

Malnutrition, *242*

Mana, *143*, **174**, *222, 231, 237, 246*

Mandarin Orange, 55, 59, 71, 72, 81, **193**

Mango, 55, 63, 81, **193**

Manifest, *247*

The Encyclopedia of Kitchen Witchery • 271

Manifestation, 56, 64, 72, *108*, *113*, *182*, *195*, *226*

Maple syrup, 48, **243**

Marigolds, **226**

Marijuana. *See* Cannabis

Marjoram, 55, 82, **135**

Marriage, *154*, *189*

Marsh Gladiolus. *See* Gladiolus

Masculine energy, *145*

Matcha, *248*

Materialization, *146*

Maternal affection, *142*

Mayocoba Bean. *See* Canary Beans

Mealie. *See* Corn

Medhika. *See* Fenugreek

Meditation, *115*, *132*, *219*, *228*, *238*, *246*, *249*

Melancholy, 47

Melegueta. *See* Grains of Paradise

Melissa. *See* Lemon Balm

Melissa Folium. *See* Lemon Balm

Melon. *See* Muskmelon

Memories, 81, *116*, *139*, *223*, *231*, *243*

Memory, *122*, *179*, *188*

Menopause, *104*, *132*, *142*, *230*

Menstrual cramps, *105*, *123*

Menstruation, *105*, *110*, *112*, *134*, *135*, *189*

Mental block, 53, *121*

Mental health, *107*, *134*, *159*, *181*

Meridian Fennel. *See* Carroway Seeds

Metabolism, *162*, *229*, *239*, *249*

Metchi. *See* Fenugreek

Mexican Chia. *See* Chia Seeds

Migraines, 85, *108*, *171*, *179*, *208*, *232*, *240*

Milk, 48, 53, 57, **243**

Milk-gowan. *See* Dandelions

Mind, *114*, *120*, *134*, *249*

Mind, balance, *107*

Mind, busy, *132*

Mind, quieten, 73

Mind, sharpen, *139*

Minerals, *182*, *235*

Mint, 53, 59, 62, 70, 81, 83, 97, **138**

Mislabeled Yams. *See* Sweet Potatoes

Mission Cact. *See* Prickly Pear

Misunderstandings, *170*

Misunderstood, *170*

Miyagawa Mandarin. *See* Naartjie

Money, *104*, *164*, *238*

Monkey Fruit. *See* Baobab

Monkey Nut. *See* Peanut

Monk's-head. *See* Dandelions

Mood, *188*, *223*

Mood disorders, 88, *115*

Mood enhancer, *120*

Morning sickness, *125*

Motherhood, *221*

Motivation, 53, 71, 80, *161*, *192*, *196*

Mountain Celery. *See* Lovage

Mouth ulcers, *112*

Moxa. *See* Mugwort

Mucus, *131*

Muggons. *See* Mugwort

Mugwort, **135**

Mulberry, **194**

Multiple sclerosis, *174*

Mums. *See* Chrysanthemums

Munjariki. *See* Basil

Muscle health, *111*, *115*, *153*, *167*,

    *235*, *245*

Muscle pain, *111*

Muscle spasms, *115*

Muskmelon, 64, 72, **194**

Musky Nut. *See* Nutmeg

Mutton, **241**

Mutual dreaming, *138*, *246*

Naartjie, **195**

Narrow-leaved Dock. *See* Sorrel

Nasturtiums, **227**

Natural instincts, *209*

Nature, 56, 58, 81, 82, *144*

Nature spirits, 83, *123*, *126*, *205*, *210*,

    *218*

Nature, connection, 82, 83

Nausea, *110*, *115*, *125*, *128*, *135*, *202*

Neep. *See* Turnip

Negative thinking, 50

Negativity, *127*, *129*, *246*

Nerve health, *153*

Nervous system, *105*, *144*, *167*

Nervousness, *104*

Neurological disorders, *115*

New project, *155*

Night terrors, *117*, *238*

Nightmares, *73*, 83, *117, 142, 144, 167, 227, 238*

Nutmeg, 48, 51, 52, 71, **135**

Nutrients, *182*

Oakwood Mushroom. *See* Shitake

Obesity, *202*

Obstacles, *165, 172, 227*

Ocimum basilicum. *See* Basil

Oil Grass. *See* Lemongrass

Old Man. *See* Mugwort, *See* Rosemary

Old Uncle Henry. *See* Mugwort

Olive, **195**

Onion, 55, 56, 88, 96, **164**

Onion Chives. *See* Chives

Oolong, 64, 73, 90, *See* Tea

Opium, *107*

Oral cancer, *198*

Oral health, *104, 112, 181, 198*

Oral health, gums, *106*

Orange, 53, 59, 61, 62, 64, 70, 71, 72, 80, 81, 97, **196**

Oregano, 49, 81, 82, 86, 91, 96, **136**

Organum. *See* Oregano

Oriental Mustard. *See* Brown Mustard

Osteoarthritis, *201*

Osteoporosis, *171, 186, 244*

Oxidative stress, *160, 174, 183, 191, 192, 194, 205, 243*

Oyster Fungus. *See* Oyster Mushroom

Oyster mushroom, **216**

Paddle Cactus. *See* Prickly Pear

Pain, 87, *130, 133, 137, 141, 147, 200, 226, 228, 231, 232, 242*

Pain relief, *104, 105*

Pain. joint, *123*

Panic, *199*

Pansy. *See* Johnny-jump-ups

Papaw. *See* Papaya

Papaya, 63, 71, **197**

Paprika, 87, **137**

Parkinson's, *174, 237*

Parsley, 81, 82, 83, **137**

Parsnip, 88, **165**

Passion, 53, 59, 61, 64, 71, 73, 81, *116, 142, 181, 196, 204, 209, 221, 223*

Passionfruit, **197**

Cassandra Sage

Past life regression, *116*

Patience, *158, See* Impatiens

Pawpaw. *See* Papaya

Peace, 73, 81, *132, 154, 166, 170, 186, 196, 226*

Peach, 60, 63, 72, 81, 91, **198**

Peanut, **210**

Pear, 53, 60, 64, 79, 81, 88, 95, **198**

Pearl Oyster Mushroom. *See* Oyster Mushroom

Peas, 53, 87, **165**

Pecan, **210**

Penny Bun. *See* Porcini mushroom

Peony, **227**

Peppermint, 83, *See* Mint

Perennial Phlox, **228**

Period pains, *128*

Perseverance, *121, 228*

Persian Cumin. *See* Carroway Seeds

Persimmon, 92, **199**

Peruano Bean. *See* Canary Beans

Pfifferling. *See* Chanterelle

Physic abilities, 64

Physical development, *193*

Physical energy, 50, 53, 59, 60, *107, 114, 130, 151, 153, 192, 223, 249*

Pickle. *See* Cucumber

Pie Plant. *See* Rhubarb

Pimento. *See* Allspice

Pimpernel. *See* Burnet

Pine, **211**

Pineapple, 55, 60, 63, 64, 81, 89, **199**

Pineapple Guave, **228**

Pistachio, **211**

Platonic love, *135*

Plums, 60, 64, 79, **200**

Pneumonia, *236*

Poise, *238*

Polar Plant. *See* Rosemary

Pomegranate, 71, 79, 81, 91, **201**

Pomelo. *See* Grapefruit

Poor Man's Saffron. *See* Marigolds

Popularity, 81, *177*

Porcini mushroom, 89, 91, **217**

Porcino. *See* Porcini mushroom

Pork, 51, 56, 93, **244**

Portabella. *See* Cremini

Portobello Mushroom. *See* Cremini

Positivity, 50, *55*, 58, *113, 226, 246*

The Encyclopedia of Kitchen Witchery • 275

Possession, *124*

Potassium, *117, 154, 167, 180*

Potato, 55, 56, 58, **167**

Poverty, *210*

Power, 55, 56, *123, 129, 160, 161, 165,*
    *186, 221, 225, 242, 246*

Precognitive abilities, *194*

Pregnancy, *151, 202, 239, 240*

Pregnant, *197*

Premenstrual, *229, 230*

Premonitions, *194*

Prickly Pear, **202**

Pride, 58

Priest's-crown. *See* Dandelions

Primrose, 61, **229**

Projects, *197*

Prophetic dreams, *223, 230, 239*

Prosperity, 59, 60, 63, 64, 73, 79, *103,*
    *108,* 110, *123, 152, 153, 154, 159, 161,*
    *164, 166, 173, 177, 180, 186, 188, 190,*
    *196, 200, 211, 212, 232, 235*

Protection, 55, 56, 58, 70, 73, 82, *109,*
    *111, 117, 120, 121, 128, 143, 147, 151,*
    *153, 159, 160, 163, 165, 168, 169, 170,*

*181, 185,* 192, *198, 201, 205, 207, 221,*
    *227, 235, 236*

Protein, *169, 235*

Pru. *See* Asparagus

Prussian Asparagus. *See*
    Asparagus

Psychic abilities, *113, 216*

Psychic ability, 61, 62, *188, 215, 223,*
    *249*

Psychic attacks, 61

Psychic awakening, 81

Psychic awareness, 53, 54, 61, 62,
    *105, 115, 124, 129, 134, 142, 144, 155,*
    *185, 240, 248*

Psychic bond, 53

Psychic connection, 54

Psychic development, 62, 81, 83, *138*

Psychic dreams, *229*

Psychic energy, *138*

Psychic healing, *185*

Psychic powers, *134*

Psychic protection, 61, *185*

Psychic vision, *135*

Psychic visions, *153, 155, 224*

Puffball. *See* Dandelions

Pumpkin, 79, **167**

Purification, *160*, *163*

Purple Bee Balm. *See* Bergamot

Purple medic. *See* Alfalfa

Queen Anne's Lace, **229**

Queen Fruit. *See* Mango

Quince, **202**

Rabbit, **244**

Rabo De Gato. *See* Hyssop

Radish, **168**

Rain dance, *123*

Raisins, *188*

Rajma. *See* Red Kidney Bean

Raspberry, 59, 63, 71, 79, 80, 81, **203**

Rebirth, *224*

Red Chili. *See* Cayenne Pepper

Red Cole. *See* Horseradish

Red Garden Beet. *See* Beetroot

Red Kidney Bean, **169**

Redness, 87

Refinement, *235*

Reinvigoration, 72

Rejection, *221*

Rejuvenation, 53, 56, 60, 64, 79, *179*

Rejuvenation, mental, *107*, 114, *131*, *136*, *138*, *159*, *181*, *184*, *185*, 245

Rejuvenation, physical, *107*, 245

Relationship, *241*

Relationship, new, *154*

Relationships, 63, *177*

Relaxation, *242*

Remembering, 70

Remembrance, 57

Ren. *See* Horseradish

Reproductive system, *201*

Resolve, 73, *181*

Respiratory illness, *135*

Respiratory issues, *110*, *131*, *232*

Restlessness, 183

Reunite, *179*

Rheindeer, **235**

Rheumatism, *111*

Rheumatoid arthritis, *201*

Rhubarb, 89, 92, **169**

Riboflavin, *242*

Riches, *197*

Ritual, *118*

Rockmelon. *See* Cantaloupe

# The Encyclopedia of Kitchen Witchery • 277

Roman Coriander. *See* Black Cumin

Romance, 70, *196*, *222*

Romarin. *See* Rosemary

Romarin Des Troubadours. *See* Rosemary

Romero. *See* Rosemary

Rooibos, 64, 93, **245**

Root Celery. *See* Celery

Rose, 73, 80, **230**

Rose de Marie. *See* Rosemary

Rose Des Marins. *See* Rosemary

Rosée De Mer. *See* Rosemary

Rosemarine. *See* Rosemary

Rosemary, 70, 81, **139**

Rusmari. *See* Rosemary

Rusmary. *See* Rosemary

Rutabaga. *See* Turnip

Sadness, 47, 81, *110*, *139*

Saffron, **140**

Safran. *See* Saffron

Sage, 49, 81, 93, **140**

Sailor's Tobacco. *See* Mugwort

Salad burnet. *See* Burnet

Salba Chia. *See* Chia Seeds

Salt, 50, 55, 56, 58, **245**

Satsuma Mandarin. *See* Naartjie

Satsuma Orange. *See* Naartjie

Sawtooth Oak Mushroom. *See* Shitake

Scallion, 55, **170**

Scarlet Bee Balm. *See* Wild Bergamot

Scurvy, *167*

Sea Lettuce. *See* Seaweed

Séance, 61, *217*

Seaweed, **246**

Second sight, *136*

Sedative, *113*, *239*

Seduction, *165*, *204*

Seer, *126*

Self-doubt, 60, 80, *143*

Self-esteem, 64, *187*, *216*

Self-love, 80

Semi-double. *See* Peony

Sénégrain. *See* Fenugreek

Sensitivity, *241*

Sensuality, *221*

Serotonin, *236*

Sesame, **141**

Sex, 53, 61, *70*, 72, 79, 83, *109*, *118*, *121*, *133*, *137*, *151*, *152*, *162*, *181*, *189*, *190*, *193*, *197*, *201*, *217*

Sexual desire, 61

Sexual stamina, *151*, *180*

Shellfish, 95, **247**

Shiitake, 58, **216**

Shyness, *118*, *153*, *159*, *201*

Sickness, *179*

Sieva Bean. *See* Butterbean

Similarity magic, *167*

Sinusitis, *112*, *127*, *128*, *131*, *145*, *162*, *168*, *171*, *172*, *181*, *185*, *190*, *197*, *200*

Skin, *115*, *123*, *130*, *181*, *189*, *191*, *195*, *197*, *203*, *204*, *205*, *211*, *236*, *245*, *247*, *250*

Skin conditions, *227*

Sleep, *107*, *115*, *130*, *132*, *133*, *143*

Sleep paralysis, *117*, *238*

Sluggish, 95

Small Burnet. *See* Burnet

Smellage. *See* Lovage

Smooth sailing, 49

Snap Beans. *See* Green Beans

Snapweed. *See* Impatiens

Snow Puff. *See* Enoki

Soft Cinnamon. *See* Ceylon Cinnamon

Sore throat, *112*, *117*, *227*, *230*, *241*

Sorrel, **141**

Sothern Pea. *See* Black-eyed peas

Soul, balance, *107*

Spanspek. *See* Cantaloupe

Spar Grass. *See* Asparagus

Sparagus. *See Asparagus*

Sparrow Grass. *See* weight loss

Sparrows Guts. *See* Asparagus

Spasms, *146*

Spearmint, 60, 70, 80, **143**

Spell casting, *124*, *125*, *133*, *151*, *165*, *205*, *246*

Sperage. *See* Aparagus

Spinach, 86, 98, **171**

Spinach Beet. *See* Beetroot

Spinach Dock. *See* Sorrel

Spirit, *195*

Spirit, busy, *132*

Spirit, communicating, 79, 81

The Encyclopedia of Kitchen Witchery • 279

Spirits, 57, 61, 81, 83, *106, 121, 122,*
   *138, 139, 143, 162, 165, 168, 180, 198,*
   *204, 224, 239*

Spirits, evil, *112, 221, 223*

Spirits, nature, *123*

Spirits, sea, *246*

Spiritual healing, 55, 73, *128*

Spontaneity, 60, 64, *201*

Spud. *See* Potato

St John's plant. *See* Mugwort

St. Josephwort. *See* Basil

Star Anise, 71, **142**

Star Aniseed. *See* Star Anise

Steinpilz. *See* Porcini mushroom

Stepfamilies, *218*

Stepsiblings, *218*

Stimulant, *120*

Stinking Gum. *See* Assafoetida

Stomach, *228, 230*

Stomach cramps, *124, 148*

Stomach problems, *125*

Stomach ulcers, *121, 130, 142, 202*

Stomach, upset, *180*

Storms, *227*

Strain, *233, 248*

Strawberry, 53, 54, 59, 60, 64, 71, 72,
   79, 80, 81, 83, 87, 90, **203**

Strength, 134, *160, 171, 207*

Strength, healing, 145

Strength, inner, *241*

Stress, 56, *107, 115,* 118, 132, *133, 134,*
   *138, 152, 184, 185, 195, 225, 226, 245*

Strife, *138*

String Beans. *See* Green beans

Stroke, 86, *126, 152, 196, 199, 203, 204*

Studies, *197*

Success, 71, *123, 128, 140, 155, 190,*
   *245*

Succubae, *143*

Suffering, *199*

Sugar, 48, 54, 93, **247**

Summoning, *172, 185*

Sunflower, **231**

Surasa. *See* Basil

Swede Turnip. *See* Turnip

Swedish Turnip. *See* Turnip

Sweet Anise. *See* Fennel

Sweet Basil. *See* Basil

Sweet Bay. *See* Bay Leaf

Sweet Cumin. *See* Anise seed

Sweet Marjoram. *See* Marjoram

Sweet Mary. *See* Lemon Balm

Sweet Melon. *See* Cantaloupe, *See* Muskmelon

Sweet Neem. *See* Curry Leaves

Sweet Peppers. *See* Bell Peppers

Sweet potato, 93, 95, **171**

Sweet Root. *See* Licorice

Sweet woodruff, 71, 86, **232**

Swelling, 87, *228*

Sword Lily. *See* Gladiolus

Sympathetic magic, *167*

Sympathy, *109*

Table Mushroom. *See* Button Mushroom

Tangerine, 95, **204**

Tarragon, 81, 88, 89, **143**

Tater. *See* Potato

Tea, **248**

Teething, 106, *134*

Temper, 57, 60, 70, *119*, *158*

Temperature, *250*

Thankfulness, *103*

Theft, *127*

Third, 62

Thoughts, calm, *71*

Thoughts, confusion, *183*

Thoughts, haunted, *131*

Thoughts, others, *111*

Thoughts, self-harming, *111*

Thoughts, sweeten, 73

Throat, sore, *138*, *178*

Thyme, 49, 56, 71, 81, 82, **144**

Thyroid, *209*, *244*

Tired, 95

Together, *183*

Togetherness, 71, 81

Tomato, **204**

Tongue-tied, *241*

Toper's plant. *See* Burnet

Tornadoes, *227*

Touch-me-not. *See* Impatiens

Toxic relationship, *183*

Tramman. *See* Elderberry

Tranquilizer, *118*

Transformation, *217*

Travel, *180*

Traveling, *138*

Trefoil. *See* Clover

Trickery, *217*

The Encyclopedia of Kitchen Witchery • 281

Trigonella. *See* Fenugreek

True Cardamom. *See* Cardamon

True Cinnamon. *See* Ceylon
Cinnamon

True Lavender. *See* Lavender

True Mustard. *See* Black Mustard

Trust, *119*

Tuberous Begonia, **232**

Tulasi. *See* HOLY BASIL

Tulpamancy, *115, 144, 242, 246*

Tulsi. *See* HOLY BASIL

Tumeric, 48, **144**

Tumors, 89

Tunrip, **172**

Uncertainty, 49

Understanding, 55, *210, 222, 232*

Understanding, people, *106*

Unfulfilled, *183*

Unity, *218, 228*

Unshu Mikan. *See* Naartjie

Unwind, *193*

Upliftment, 80

Urinary tract, *183, 225*

Urucum. *See* Annatto seed

Valentine's day, *193*

Vanatulasi. *See* Basil

Vanilla, 52, 81, *See* Vanilla beans

Vanilla beans, 64, 70, 73, **145**

Varicose veins, *227*

Varvara. *See* Basil

Vascular system, *246*

Vegetable Mustard. *See* Brown
Mustard

Venison. *See* Buck

Vibrations, negative, 50, 55, 56, *246*

Vibrations, positive, 57

Victory, 71, *232*

Vigor, *227*

Viola. *See* Violets

Violets, **233**

Viral infection, *134*

Virility, *158*

Vision, *155*

Visva Tulsi. *See*

Vitality, 48, 50, 53, *145, 225, 227, 243*

Vitamin A, *153, 184, 242*

Vitamin B, *218, 242*

Vitamin B12, *242*

Vitamin C, *117, 118, 167, 191*

Vitamin D, 86, *215, 216*

Vitamins, *182*, *235*

Walnut, 87, 91, 94, **211**

War, *138*

Warm heart, 51, 52, 57, 81

Warmth, 48

Wasabi, **146**

Water, 54, **249**

Water retention, *118*

Watermelon, 61, 72, **205**

Wax Bean. *See* Butterbean

Wealth, 49, *109*, *140*, *168*, *181*, *189*, *197*, *201*

Wedding, *189*, *193*

Weed. *See* Cannabis

Weight gain, 88, *243*

Weight loss, 88, *118*, *120*, *129*, *146*, *151*, *158*, *160*, *163*, *178*, *180*, *188*, *191*, *195*, *199*, *217*, *229*, *248*, *250*

Weight management, *156*

Wellbeing, *249*

Well-being, emotional, *187*

White blood cells, *216*

White Button. *See* Cremini

White Button Mushroom. *See* Button Mushroom

White Honeysuckle. *See* Honeysuckle

White Horehound. *See* Horehound

White Mustard, **146**

White tea, 64, 73, 90, *See* Tea

Whooping cough, *110*

Wild Baby's Breath. *See* Sweet Woodruff

Wild Bachelor's Button. *See* Chicory

Wild Bergamot, **110**

Wild Carrot. *See* Queen Anne's Lace

Wild Chives. *See* Chives

Wild Marjoram. *See* Oregano

Wild Pansy. *See* Johnny-jump-ups

Wild Purple Bergamot. *See* Bergamot

Wild Wormwood. *See* Mugwort

Willpower, 50, 59, *155*

Wineberry. *See* Gooseberry

Winter Mushrooms. *See* Enoki

Wisdom, 49, 60, 64, 73, 79, 81, *141*, *160*, *169*, *196*, *198*, *207*, *209*, *210*, *233*

Wishing, 71, *103*, *108*, *192*, *201*

Witch-gowan. *See* Dandelions

Wits, *201*

Womanhood rituals, *163*

Womb, *186*

Woo Lu Bar. *See* Fenugreek

Wounds, *201*

Wyrmwort. *See* Tarragon

Yam, 89, 93, **172**

Yellow Chanterelle. *See*

    Chanterelle

Yellow Mustard. *See* White

    Mustard

Yellow-gowan. *See* Dandelions

Youth, *229*

Youthfulness, 61, *211*, *250*

Ysop. *See* Hyssop

Zafran. *See* Saffron

Zobo Pepper. *See* Cloves

Zucchini, **173**

Printed in the USA
CPSIA information can be obtained
at www.ICGtesting.com
LVHW022019151024
793894LV00009B/258